HAPPY ABOUT My JOB Search

How to Conduct an Effective Job Search
for a More Successful Career

BARBARA SAFANI

Happy About

Copyright © 2012 by BARBARA Safani

All rights reserved. No part of this book shall be reproduced, stored in a retrieval system, or transmitted by any means electronic, mechanical, photocopying, recording, or otherwise without written permission from the publisher.

Published by Happy About®
20660 Stevens Creek Blvd., Suite 210,
Cupertino, CA 95014

http://happyabout.com

First Printing: November 2012
Paperback ISBN: 978-1-60005-224-8 (1-60005-224-X)
eBook ISBN: 978-1-60005-225-5 (1-60005-225-8)

Place of Publication: Silicon Valley, California, USA
Paperback Library of Congress Number: 2012953065

Trademarks
All terms mentioned in this book that are known to be trademarks or service marks have been appropriately capitalized. Neither Happy About®, nor any of its imprints, can attest to the accuracy of this information. Use of a term in this book should not be regarded as affecting the validity of any trademark or service mark.

Warning and Disclaimer
Every effort has been made to make this book as complete and as accurate as possible. The information provided is on an "as is" basis. The author(s), publisher, and their agents assume no responsibility for errors or omissions. Nor do they assume liability or responsibility to any person or entity with respect to any loss or damages arising from the use of information contained herein.

"Barbara Safani has pulled together a toolkit of job search tips that readers at every professional level can benefit from. The advice on resumes, networking, interviewing, and salary negotiation is practical and immediately actionable. Job seekers can quickly improve their engagement with recruiters and hiring authorities by implementing many of the suggestions Safani recommends."

~ Edward Fleischman, CEO, The Execu|Search Group

"Barbara Safani hits it again! Her relevant, practical advice and thought-provoking questions and situations to ponder offer the most effective career coaching expertise in the market! As someone who has been interacting with job seekers on a daily basis for the last decade, I couldn't agree more with all her commentary and counsel. She's right on and her strategies and suggestions apply to a broad range of job seekers across industries, levels, or areas of expertise. It's a must-read for anyone thinking of making a job change or transition!"

~ Lorri Zelman, Managing Director, Human Resources Practice, Solomon Page Group

"Safani has done it again ... zeroed in on the most important (and most current) job search how-to's that are rooted in actual job seekers' successes. With these tips delivered in short, succinct, 'bite-sized' pieces, you'll find it easy to take action and gain momentum in your search. Bravo!"

~ Susan Whitcomb, author of Resume Magic, Interview Magic, and The Twitter Job Search Guide

"As a career professional with over twenty-five years of experience, I always approach new books with the thought, 'tell me something I don't know already.' I must say, when I was asked to review this book I expected that I would find things that I never thought of. Barbara, who has presented at Pace, has encyclopedic knowledge of the job search and strategy process. In fact, I would call this book the 'encyclopedia of job search and strategy.' The book is full of tips, 'to-do's,' and 'not-to-do's' for every phase of the job search process.

"It starts with a discussion of job boards, unrealistic expectations, branding, and standing out, and continues with resumes, networking, using social media sites, and interviewing. The book is loaded with specific examples and uses humor throughout.

"I would highly recommend this book for job seekers from graduating students to experienced professionals."

~ Barry Miller, PhD, Manager,
New Employer Development, Pace University

Barbara Safani

DEDICATION

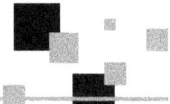

To my mom. I've watched you since I was a little girl embrace and master new skills in each of your jobs. Your continuous curiosity and willingness to learn taught me to be equally open-minded and inquisitive as my own career evolved.

ACKNOWLEDGMENTS

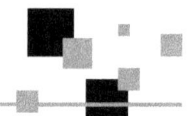

I would like to thank all the people who have shared their career journeys with me over the years. Your willingness to report on your struggles and successes was the inspiration for much of this book and I have gained so much wisdom from your stories and inspiration from your resilience. I would also like to thank my publisher, Mitchell Levy, for continuing to provide such a supportive environment for my ideas, my editor, Karen Silvestri for her red pen magic, and production director Liz Tadman for keeping this project on task.

A Message from Happy About®

Thank you for your purchase of this Happy About book. It is available online at *http://happyabout.info/social-media-success.php* or at other online and physical bookstores.

- Please contact us for quantity discounts at sales@happyabout.info
- If you want to be informed by email of upcoming Happy About® books, please email *bookupdate@happyabout.info*

Happy About is interested in you if you are an author who would like to submit a non-fiction book proposal or a corporation that would like o have a book written for you. Please contact us by emaileditorial@happyabout.info or phone (1-408-257-3000).

Other Happy About books available include:

- Happy About My Resume
  http://www.happyabout.com/affiliates/myresume.php
- #JOBSEARCHtweet Book01
  http://www.happyabout.com/affiliates/jobsearchtweet01.php
- I'm at a Networking Event-Now What???
  http://www.happyabout.com/affiliates/networking-event.php
- I Need to Brand My Story Online and Offline-Now What???
  http://www.happyabout.com/affiliates/storytelling.php

TABLE of CONTENTS

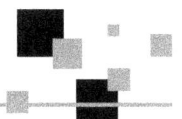

Chapter One: Job Seekers Are a Lot like 450 Pound Pianos: General Job Search Etiquette and Advice 1
   Beating the Job Search Blues 1
   Stop Complaining About Your Job Search 2
   8 Things Recruiters Want Job Seekers to Know 3
   5 Alternatives to Posting to a Job Board 4
   Job Seekers Are a Lot like 450 Pound Pianos 5
   Do New Year's Resolutions Have to Happen on
      New Year's? 7
   How to Land a Job Without a Four-Year Degree 9
   Defy Gravity to Land Safely in Your Next Job 10
   Keep a Job Search "To Do" List 12
   Top 10 Mistakes Job Seekers Make 13
   How to Protect Your Career if a Tornado Hits 15
   Job Seekers: You Are Fooling Yourself If. 16
   Making the Job Search Fun 17
   Let The Job Search Begin! 18
   5 Things Not to Say to a Job Seeker during
      the Holiday Season 19
   10 Things to Do Before the Pink Slip Arrives 20
   Email Etiquette During a Job Search 22
   Is Age Really What's Holding You Back? 23
   6 Common Job Search Mistakes 24
   5 Ways to Lose Your Job in the Electronic Age 25
   Is Your Name Hurting Your Chances of Landing a Job? 26
   How Many Americans Are Happy at Work? 28
   Would You Marry Someone Who Was Unemployed? 28
   Changing Careers: Look Before You Leap 29
   Career Advice from My Dad 31
   The Future of the Job Search 32
   Top Career Mistakes Boomers Make Online 35
   20 Ways to Get a Job 36

10 Ways a Stay-at-Home Mom Can Stay in the
    Professional Loop 40
The First 100 Days in a New Job 43
5 Questions to Ask Yourself before Going Back to
    School for an MBA 44

Chapter Two: Is Your Resume a Turkey? Tips for Building More Powerful Resumes and Cover Letters 47

How Long Should My Resume Be? 47
What are Resume Keywords? 49
How to Fix Four Common Resume Mistakes 51
Does Your Resume Font Matter? 54
Writing a Resume That Cuts to the Chase 55
10 Reasons to Use a Resume Template (Not!) 57
Seven Things You Don't Want to Have
    on Your Resume 58
How to Communicate Difficult Stories
    on Your Resume 59
Resume Writing Tips for Susan Lucci and Others Who
    Haven't Looked for a Job in Forty Years 60
Phrases That Kill Resumes 63
Is Your Resume a Turkey? 64
Resume Renovations 65
Create an Authentic and Ethical Resume
    to Win the Job 66
Does Your Resume Make You Look Like
    A Job Hopper? 68
One Typo You Should Have on Your Resume 69
5 Resume Formatting Mistakes to Avoid 70
5 Resume Tricks That Will Make You Stand Out 71
Questions to Ask Yourself Before Writing Your Resume 73
How to Address Employment Gaps on a Resume 75
Functional Resumes Should be Re-Named
    Dysfunctional Resumes 76
4 Tips for Career Change Cover Letters 77
Do You Need a Cover Letter? 78
10 Tips for Writing Stand-Out Cover Letters 79
Forget the Thank You Letter, Lose the Job 80

Is It Acceptable to Send a Thank You Letter Via Email? 81
How to Write a Reference List 82
I'm Afraid to List My Former Boss as a Reference 83
What's Holding You Back from Writing a
    Better Resume? 84
6 Ways to Fix Resume Formatting Mistakes
    and Save Space 87
4 Ways to Source Keywords for Your Resume 88

Chapter Three: Five Networking Lessons I Wish I'd Learned in High School: Advice on How to Strengthen the Quality of Your Network and Network More Strategically 91

Networking With a School or Corporate
    Alumni Connection 91
10 Tips for Helping Your Child Land His First
    Job Out of College 93
LinkedIn Tips 95
LinkedIn Invites: When a Potential Connection Quickly
    Becomes a Disconnect 98
Status Update - I'm Still Looking for Work 99
Networking Your Way to Your Next Job 101
Online Networking Tips for Job Search 102
Do I Ever Think About You if We Aren't Connected
    Online? 104
World Trade Center Memories from the Bridge 105
Creepy Networking 106
Networking Basics 107
Why Networking Gets a Bad Rap and What to Do
    About It 108
Holiday Networking Can Facilitate New Year
    Opportunities 111
Five Networking Lessons I Wish I'd
    Learned in High School 112
Volunteering as a Career Management Strategy 114
In Networking, Sometimes a Conversation about
    Nothing is Something 115
Ideas for Face-to-Face Networking 116

Tips for Building Visibility at Professional Development Meetings 117
The Healing Power of Social Networking 118
Top Excuses for Not Networking.. 119
Accelerate Your Networking during the Slow Summer Months 120
Make Your Network Work for You 122
I Just Landed a New Job So I'm Done Networking, Right?.. 123
Networking: Mind Your Manners... 124
5 Ways to Use Facebook for Your Job Search....................... 125

Chapter Four: Interview Mistakes Straight From American Idol: The Dos and Don'ts of Interviewing 127

Can't Remember the Last Time You Went on a Job Interview? 127
Focus on the Things You Can Control................................... 128
Interview Mistakes Straight From American Idol................. 129
What Not to Wear to the Interview 130
Look for Clues to Uncover the Corporate Culture................ 131
Interviews…Get by With a Little Help from Your Friends 133
Take a Ride in the Elevator before You Interview 134
What Your Grandparents Can Teach You about Interviewing 135
How to Stand Out in a Panel Interview.................................. 137
Mastering the Phone Interview.. 138
Could Your Interview Style Use a Seven Second Delay?... 140
Common Interview Questions and What They Mean 141
How to Handle "Inappropriate" Interview Questions 144
Interview Questions for Recent College Grads 145
What is Your Weakness and Other Tough Interview Questions 146
24 Interview Tips That Help Make a Great First Impression 149

6 Tips for Following Up after the Interview	151
6 Strategies for Gathering Salary Information	152
5 Suggestions for Better Salary Negotiation Conversations	153
7 Tips for Salary Negotiation	154
Show Me the Money!	156
About the Author:	157
Other Happy About Books	158

FOREWORD

Let's look at the facts:

1. Today's job search has become a remarkably complex process, and everyone needs help navigating the new hiring landscape.

2. Job seekers must be savvy in BOTH traditional job search activities and social media tools and hiring technologies.

3. Competition for every position is fierce. It's not just 20 people applying; it's 200 people.

4. Many of those people are as well qualified as you are, so you MUST distinguish yourself within the market and showcase your most valuable achievements.

So, what are the solutions? What can you do to position yourself ahead of the competition?

In Happy About My Job Search, my long-time colleague and friend, Barbara Safani, tells you what you need to know and how to use that information to win in today's employment market. Her advice is valuable whether your search is around the corner, in another state, or a continent away.

Using a series of short sections that address scores of very specific job search and career management topics, Barb gives you a roadmap to follow in an easy and enjoyable read. Her advice is clear, concise, and—most important—actionable.

And, bottom line, that's what a successful job search is all about… taking action to move your career forward, position yourself as the best candidate, and capture the opportunities you want.

Heed Barb's recommendations, follow her instructions, listen to her lessons, and enjoy her stories as you move forward in achieving your own career dreams!

Wendy S. Enelow, CCM, MRW, JCTC, CPRW
Author, Trainer, & Career Consultant
Executive Director, Career Thought Leaders Consortium
Executive Director, Resume Writing Academy

Barbara Safani

CHAPTER 1

Job Seekers Are a Lot like 450 Pound Pianos: General Job Search Etiquette and Advice

Job search is a process that requires time, patience, and self-reflection. It forces you to stretch, take risks, be gracious, and often think about others more than you think about yourself. It is an emotional experience, but one that can help you grow, gain confidence, and build a better future for yourself. This chapter focuses on general job search concepts to help you understand the process, create an accountability plan, and keep you motivated along the way.

Beating the Job Search Blues

My clients frequently ask me for advice on how to stay positive during a job search. Here are my top five tips.

1. **Find an accountability partner.** Find another person in a job search to share advice and leads with and help you get back up when you are down. Partner with someone who you will not be competing with for job leads... perhaps someone more junior or more senior than you, or someone in a different industry or job function. Sharing strategies and feelings with someone who is going through the same thing as you can be extremely therapeutic.

2. **Keep a job search journal.** Record your search and make special mentions of how you are feeling on your up days. This will remind you on your down days that you will have up days again. A journal can also help you track patterns in your job search campaign that have contributed to both up and down days. Once you recognize the patterns, you can make the necessary adjustments to your search strategy.

3. **Join a support group for job seekers.** This might be a Meet Up group (www.meetup.com) or community group or a professional association that

has a special interest group for members in transition. These groups are great for building your network, sharing leads, and staying current on job search and industry information.

4. **Think about those less fortunate than you.** Find ways to give back to your personal and professional communities through volunteer work. It is a rewarding way to show good will and build networking relationships in the process. It will also help remind you that even though you are in job search mode, there are many things in your life to be thankful for.

5. **Enjoy your family.** While job searching is a full-time job in itself, it does afford you some flexibility in how you plan your day. Take advantage of your flex schedule to attend a child's soccer game or go to lunch with a spouse.

Stop Complaining About Your Job Search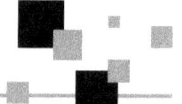

There are many things to complain about in a job search. It can be a frustrating process. However, complaining doesn't help you land a job any faster. Here are some common job search complaints and some strategies for moving forward.

1. **My resume isn't working.** When job seekers don't get interviews, they often blame the resume. While it's true that an achievement-driven resume helps position job seekers for interviews, the resume is just one piece of the process. If you are complaining about your resume, examine how you are using that resume and change your behavior if necessary. If your primary method of searching is posting on job boards and you aren't getting results, start building meaningful connections with the people who can hire you rather than the people who are parsing the resume data. Create a proactive plan to target companies that you would like to work for where you believe there is a good fit and approach them directly, whether they are actively recruiting or not. Every company recruits at some point…build relationships now so you are considered as a candidate when an opportunity presents itself.

2. **No one in my network can help me find a job.** Why is that? Have you spent the last 15 years talking to the same three colleagues or have you extended your networking efforts to include friends, family, school alumni, past colleagues, members of professional organizations, community service providers, and members of online networking communities? Not everyone can help you in a job search; you need to have a robust network, so you are not relying on the same three people for introductions.

3. **I interviewed for a position and I haven't heard back about next steps.** Take the initiative to follow up on your own. This doesn't mean leaving dozens of voicemail messages or sending multiple emails. Become top of the potential employer's mind by sending a reminder of the value you could bring to the team. This might be a relevant article, information about an industry event, or an acknowledgement of something you read about the company recently.

4. **It takes so long for the companies to make a hiring decision.** Get used to it. While we would like to think that we are the #1 priority for hiring authorities, we often aren't. General business issues, workplace snafus, and shifting priorities can all effect when the hiring decision is made. Deal with it by reaching out periodically to communicate that you are aware that they haven't made a decision yet but you continue to remain very interested in the position.

5. **The person who interviewed me doesn't seem to "get" what I do.** If your first interview is with a human resources professional, that person may recruit for several functions across the company and not know all the nuts and bolts of what you do. They may still represent a bridge to the next round of interviews, so keep an open mind and a positive demeanor. Generally, HR is looking for a cultural fit and your ability to work well in a team, so be sure to have several accomplishment-focused stories to demonstrate these competencies.

8 Things Recruiters Want Job Seekers to Know

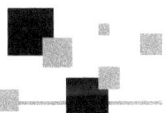

I chat with recruiters frequently and I often ask them this question:

"If you could tell job seekers one thing, what would it be?" Here are their top responses.

1. **Be transparent.** If there is a gap on your resume, explain it on the document itself. If you don't explain the reason for the gap, we will draw our own conclusions.

2. **Use a chronological format over a functional format.** We will assume you are hiding something if you submit a purely functional resume. Recruiters need to understand all the movement in your career. If dates are missing or if your resume focuses too much on functional skills to downplay the chronology, we will become suspicious.

3. **Don't apply to every job posting.** Only apply to those jobs for which you truly meet the qualifications. Applying to jobs you are not qualified for is a waste of both your time and ours.

4. **Don't call incessantly to follow up on a job posting.** If you don't hear from me, I have nothing to tell you.

5. **Drop the resume objective.** Include a summary on your resume explaining how you can add value to the organization, rather than an objective explaining what you are looking for. Hiring managers aren't interested in what you are looking for; they are interested in people who can solve their business problems.

6. **Add a competency or skills section to your resume.** Make it easy to figure out what your core skills are. We need to know right away if you have the basic skill set to do the job.

7. **Get rid of the entitlement act.** Don't assume you will get a certain salary just because you ask for it. We are willing to negotiate if it is within our budget.

8. **Don't upload a Microsoft Word document into the text box of our job site.** We can't read it. The formatting is severely compromised when you do this and we will ignore your application. Instead, convert your Word document to a text only file.

Building relationships with recruiters is one way to get closer to landing your next job. If you can learn to appreciate their needs, you will increase your chances of landing more interviews.

5 Alternatives to Posting to a Job Board

Every day I speak to job seekers who use the job boards as their main method of search and get minimal results. Rather than spending the majority of your time on a search strategy that tends to yield a very low return on the investment of your time, try some alternative methods to find people to help you with your search. Here are a few suggestions.

1. Go around the gatekeeper. If you find an open position through a job board or company website, don't only submit your resume to human resources—they're often gatekeepers who don't have much control over who ends up getting hired. Instead, go around the gatekeeper and do some Internet research to find the hiring manager or other decision maker and market your candidacy directly to them rather than being one of the "sheep" using the job boards.

2. Cybersleuth your way to decision makers. Perform keyword searches for companies, job title, etc. on Google and LinkedIn to see if you can find someone in your network connected to the company you want to get into or to request an introduction. Use the More Insights feature on company pages of LinkedIn to track movement of employees at a target company and spot potential opportunities. Check out Jigsaw to source company contact information including phone numbers and email addresses for a nominal fee.

3. Become a stalker (sort of). Once you find people who are connected to the industries and companies you are interested in, do some research to find out more about them. Do they belong to certain professional associations or the local golf club or do they attend events for certain charities? Perhaps you should be in those professional and social circles too…and maybe you could "serendipitously" meet them at an event.

4. Tweet your stuff. Twitter is not about telling everyone what you had for lunch. It is about creating authentic and consistent messaging about who you are and what you know. Set up a profile (it's easy and free) and start "tweeting" about things related to your professional expertise. Share links to articles that are relevant for the types of people you are trying to attract and give shout outs to others by "re-tweeting" information from them that you think others could benefit from. Use Twitter Search to find other people with common interests and professions that you should be following.

5. Research industries and job functions that are trending up. Check out the Occupational Outlook Handbook (www.bls.gov/ooh/) to learn more about industries and job functions predicted to experience growth over the next decade.

Job Seekers Are a Lot Like 450 lb. Pianos

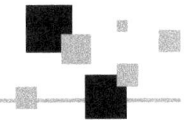

Last year, I had a piano delivered to my house. Arranging for a piano delivery is no small feat. Besides making arrangements with the showroom, I had to coordinate the insurance with my apartment building's managing agent and figure out if the piano would fit in my elevator. Delivering a baby seemed to be much easier than this ordeal.

The delivery was scheduled for a Wednesday, yet the piano showed up at my house on Tuesday. It seems that the employee from the piano showroom missed one minor detail…recording and communicating the correct delivery date to the movers. The piano arrived just as I was leaving my house for a meeting, so I had to refuse delivery and send the piano back to the showroom.

Ok, we're all human and we all make mistakes. However, in some situations you are going to be judged more harshly than others. If a delivery of new sheets or towels showed up on the wrong day, I might not have given it a second thought. But it's hard to shrug off the fact that a 450 lb piano showed up on my doorstep unannounced. Even if the employee at the showroom is the employee of the year every year and is frequently praised for her attention to detail, to me she will always be "the lady who delivered a piano to my house on the wrong day."

Job searching is a situation where your actions are under a microscope. Errors that might be passed over in your day-to-day work are scrutinized much more diligently when hiring managers are reviewing applicants. When you start the job search process, an employer doesn't know you and they don't trust you yet. They don't know if you are competent to do the job, so each of your interactions with them either builds that trust or destroys it. Here are a few errors that job seekers often make and are frequently judged by.

- **Resume typos…**It's very rare that I receive an email without a typo. I see typos on websites and blogs all the time. It doesn't really color my opinion of that person. However, in a job search, typos on the resume make a red flag go up for many hiring managers. The concern is that if the applicant wasn't detail-oriented enough to catch the typos in their resume, they may make other, more costly errors for the company.

- **Fashion Faux pas…**Everyone has showed up at work at some point in time in some outfit that was far from flattering, too casual, inconsistent with the company's corporate culture, or even offensive. In most cases, the fashion faux pas becomes fodder for the water cooler for a day or two and then just goes away. But on an interview, the candidate quickly turns into "the applicant in the fishnet stockings" or "the guy with the really bad tie" and again a judgment is passed. The concern is that based on the applicant's dress they won't fit in with the company's culture or perhaps lack sound judgment in other areas.

- **Arriving late to the interview…** Just about everyone has been late to work at one time or another. Unless it becomes a chronic issue, it is generally accepted and not a big deal. However, on an interview, arriving late can signal to a hiring manager that you are not reliable or dependable or that you don't manage your time well.

- **Electronic whoops…**We've all been in situations where someone's cell phone rings during a presentation or important meeting. Maybe it's a bit embarrassing, but it's quickly forgotten. However, if your phone rings during an interview, the interviewer notices and may pass a judgment about you or even your consideration of others.

When you apply for a job, you are a lot like a 450 lb piano. Everything you do is obvious. Everything you do gets noticed. Little errors in your job search strategy can quickly turn into detrimental ones. The person who arranged for my piano delivery should have checked and double checked the delivery date...because it's a piano. Job seekers need to check and recheck all the little details that go into an effective job search...because it's your career. Both are really big things that you don't want to screw up.

Do New Year's Resolutions Have to Happen on New Year's?

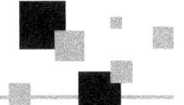

After the holidays, people start to talk about their New Year's resolutions...lose weight, exercise more, quit smoking, get out of debt, and find a new job are the ones I hear most frequently. And while I think that New Year's resolutions are a great idea in theory, I think that a lot of people fail to keep their New Year's resolutions because often the only criteria motivating the person to make the resolution is the time of year.

One year I made several big changes in my life. Yet none of them happened overnight. Some took months to make, others took years, and one took more than a decade to come to terms with. None of them was motivated by the time of year. They were motivated by a feeling that I could no longer continue in a situation under the current circumstances or by the fact that I wanted something and I wanted it sooner rather than later. Basically, my desire to change a situation was greater than my desire not to change it. There really wasn't an "aha moment" or even a calculated plan in many cases; the changes happened because in my mind, they had to at one point or another.

The other thing about my changes was that few of them went smoothly and most had a "one step forward, two steps back" feel to them. Nevertheless, I was able to persevere because I didn't link the changes to a time frame. With New Year's resolutions, people often link them to a time frame, and if the person can't follow the timeline, they frequently abandon the new behavior before they can see the true results of their efforts.

So, if one of your New Year's resolutions is to find a new job, here are some suggestions for forgetting about the time of year and instead focusing on the long term change.

1. **Don't declare a New Year's resolution; instead, set a long-term goal with some interim milestones.** If you know you would like to change jobs at some point in time or land a job as quickly as possible, commit to five things you could do over the next month to move towards that goal. That may mean setting up informational interviews, joining a professional association, becoming more active on social media sites, or starting your own job search group. Do something to move yourself closer to your goal.

2. **Don't create a defined time frame for achieving the goal.** Forget the formulas about how long a typical job search lasts. There is no such thing as a typical job search. Think about nurturing existing relationships and building new ones to gather information, extend your professional visibility, and secure more interviews. Build relationships whenever you can. Graciously accept a meeting whether it will occur next week or next month.

3. **Don't reset the clock when your progress towards your goal feels stagnant.** Some weeks your search will feel like you are slogging through mud or sinking in quicksand. Other weeks will be more fruitful. A slow week doesn't mean the market has tanked or everyone must be on vacation. Don't give up during the slow times; instead, use the downtime to focus on other aspects of your search such as improving your resume or creating a target list of companies to explore...keep on keeping on.

4. **Don't blame external factors for your inability to change; look inward to figure out why you can't change just yet.** It's easy to blame a bad economy for your lack of progress. However, often it's our own insecurities that hold us back. Even when people want to find a new job or land a job when they don't have one, it can still be hard. Maybe it's fear of rejection, apprehension about taking a risk, or a feeling that maybe the grass really isn't greener on the other side. It's okay (and normal) to have these feelings. Explore them, deal with them and make decisions as to whether your desire to change exceeds these feelings at this point in time.

5. **Cut yourself some slack if you don't reach your goal as quickly as you would like to.** We are all impatient at times. Yet the job market often doesn't take this into account. In an employer's market, searches tend to last a long time and it's not unusual to go through several rounds of interviews over several months before a hiring decision is made. You can't control every aspect of your search. Focus on what you can control and recognize that things might take longer than you would like.

Forget the one time resolution on January 1. Instead, focus on contributing something towards your career each and every day...that's what career management is all about.

How to Land a Job without a Four-Year Degree

I once listened in on a recruiter panel where an HR person from a Fortune 500 company admitted that he added a Bachelor's degree to the list of requirements for all his job postings because it was an easy way to screen out candidates.

He didn't try to make the case that the degree is a key predictor of success in corporate jobs, an argument you often hear. He was honest in saying that the requirement was just a way to widdle out candidates in a competitive job market.

He's not alone in this practice and it presents a challenge for job seekers who lack the crucial piece of parchment.

I meet many job seekers who are very concerned with the fact that they lack a four-year degree. Many often express regret, guilt, and even shame over not having one. They seem to have bought into the idea that without the degree, they either aren't qualified for the position or don't stand a chance at landing it. This is not necessarily the case. The real issue is that they are dealing with a gatekeeper who has put up an obstacle that they can't get past. However, the solution isn't to give up or decide that the gatekeeper must be right; the solution is to go around the gatekeeper and find another door for entry.

I often write about the fact that most people get their jobs through their network. When there is an obstacle in the way of your search, your network becomes even more crucial. Therefore, if a lack of a college degree is the obstacle, getting the degree isn't necessarily the most efficient way around the obstacle. Here are a few things to consider.

- Rather than trying to get past a job board with a structured set of requirements, try to find an insider at the company who can advocate for you and let the decision maker know all you have to offer. Try every possible angle; talk to friends and family, reach out to colleagues and people you know through affinity groups, and search your contacts on LinkedIn and Facebook to find an in at the company. Once there is someone advocating for your candidacy and singing your praises, your academic credentials rarely become an important factor in granting an interview.

- If you have any college credits, list the university and area of study on your resume to show you have some college experience. If you have more than one year of college, you may want to list the number of credits you have as well.

- If you have licenses, certifications, or training classes that are relevant to your target audience, list them on the resume to show your dedication to continuing to gain knowledge in your area of expertise.

- When interviewing, showcase stories that prove you have been successful in your previous roles. Maybe it's a story about being the top sales person, the accountant who reaped the greatest savings for the company, the HR manager with the best time-to-hire metrics, or the self-made CEO who led the company from being in the red to multimillion-dollar profits. Your recent professional accomplishments generally have more relevancy than educational accomplishments achieved decades ago.

- During an interview, ask if there are any concerns about your candidacy to see if the hiring manager brings up your education. If they do, discuss how you have performed as well as or even better than your colleagues with a degree. Maybe you trained colleagues who had more formal education than you on a particular product or were selected to lead a project over your teammates despite not having a degree. Prove how your lack of a degree was not an impediment to doing your job well.

I learned a long time ago that education is not necessarily correlated with success in a job. I have read the success stories of corporate icons such as Bill Gates, Michael Dell, Richard Branson, Barry Diller, and Mark Zuckerberg, all who never graduated from college. If you have been struggling with your search and believe that your lack of a degree is creating a roadblock, try going down a different path to find the right contacts that can help you land your next gig.

Defy Gravity to Land Safely in Your Next Job

I think that everyone who is in a job search has to defy gravity in order to gain traction, particularly in a competitive job market such as the one we are facing right now. You need to take a leap of faith, step outside your comfort zone, and do things differently. Because techniques that worked during your last job search might not work today. Here are my five gravity defying recommendations to help you take that leap and still land safely.

- **Don't pull out your most recent resume, slap on your last position, and call that an update.** Stop treating your resume like another piece of paper that needs to be in your briefcase when you start interviewing and start acknowledging it for what it is, a marketing tool and advertisement for "brand you". Forget about what you think are the rules around resume writing. I have news for you, there really aren't any. The goal is to make a powerful and memorable impression, quickly and with whatever it takes. This can be achieved by communicating your impact on the organizations you have supported and it can be proven with stories, visuals, case studies, testimonials, or links to podcasts, whitepapers, and even YouTube videos. Resumes that read like job descriptions won't cut it; they will never defy gravity, but instead will fall flat with the hiring manager.

- **Get off the job boards.** Job boards cater to the most complacent of job seekers, the ones who expect the jobs to come to them. The ones who think that if they throw enough resumes against the job board wall, one of them is bound to stick. But it doesn't really work that way because the person on the other side of that job board is getting resumes hurled at them much faster than they can catch them. So they are forced to use applicant tracking software to parse the data in your resume and reduce its substance down to a few keywords. Keywords don't really communicate success. In addition, while that hiring manager is trying to field all the applicants from the job boards, they are also building relationships via other channels. Let's face it; if someone they know introduces them to a candidate, there is a much greater likelihood that they will check out that candidate first and actually look at their resume while the applicant tracking system does all the grunt work parsing data on the other 500 applicants. Which set of eyes would you rather be in front of, the human eye or the computer one?

- **Don't expect a recruiter to find you your next job.** Even a recruiter will tell you that you are more likely to find your next position through a connection than through them. Just because you found your last job via a recruiter, it doesn't mean you will land your next job the same way. Recruiters are inundated with prospects but don't necessarily have the inventory of job openings to match the demand. Build your network by becoming an active member of professional and personal communities to extend your visibility and circle of influence. Break away from a reliance on recruiters and start making things happen on your own.

- **Don't turn your back on social media.** I've heard all the excuses. If you don't think that social media is relevant to you in a job search, watch how quickly you become irrelevant to the many decision makers using it to find top talent. Dip your toe in the social media water, start some conversations, support others, and learn how to protect your privacy to alleviate any concerns you have about using these tools.

- **Don't purchase a book on interviewing and expect to interview well.** Interview books can help you lay the foundation for your interview strategy, but they can't tell you how you should answer the interview questions. A strong interview strategy is one that communicates your unique value proposition through stories of success. Review interview questions to determine the underlying competency the hiring manager is searching for. Then showcase an example of something you did in the past that proves you have that competency. This strategy builds your credibility and helps the hiring manager gain trust in your abilities. You will never wow a hiring manager by regurgitating the pat answer listed on page 23 of some interview book.

Defying gravity in your job search takes a lot of work and it requires some risk. But if the old methods of job search aren't working for you, then you need to try something new.

Keep a Job Search "To Do" List

Many of my clients tell me that one of the difficulties in a job search is that there is often no way to gage daily success, and job seekers often wonder if they are being productive and conducting their search in the most efficient manner.

In order to feel productive and not wonder if you are simply "spinning your wheels," I recommend setting daily and weekly goals for your campaign. These goals will help you remain focused and motivated and will help you realize the small successes that can eventually lead to a larger success in conjunction with your job search. Here are some examples of weekly goals.

1. Set up at least 2 networking meetings
2. Research 10 target companies
3. Follow up on 10 cold calls made the week before
4. Search for and follow up on 10 potential contacts on LinkedIn
5. Offer at least one hour of your time in a volunteer capacity
6. Attend at least one professional networking event
7. Attend at least one social networking event
8. Spend one hour per week monitoring aggregate and niche job boards
9. Complete one marketing document (i.e. resume, bio, personal marketing plan)
10. Do at least one non job search activity that is just for you

Keep track of daily and weekly progress by either keeping a journal or using a job search contact and information management tool such as Jibber Jobber (www.jibberjobber.com) or Job Katch (www.jobkatch.com). This strategy will help you monitor progress on each activity, make decisions about what is working and what is not, and uncover where you need to spend more or less time.

View looking for your job as your full time job for now and plan to spend 35 hours per week working your search. Stay focused on your activity list and hold yourself accountable for its completion. Partner with someone else in search if you think you need someone to keep you on track and give you a gentle nudge.

If you are consistently incorporating these types of tasks into your search campaign, you are making progress towards your end goal. It is the consistency of the activities that often leads to the opened door, finding the needle in the haystack job spec, or reconnecting with the colleague you thought you would never hear from again. If you need affirmation that you are on the right track, find a local job search support group to hear what others are doing and share new ideas and best practices.

Top 10 Mistakes Job Seekers Make

1. **Inflate their qualifications or lie on their resume.** While a resume is not a legal document, it should be an accurate representation of your experience and achievements. I advocate for showing your employment history in the best possible light, buy lying is never wise.

2. **Forget to proofread their resume.** One of the easiest ways to show an employer you don't pay much attention to details is to submit a resume with a typo. Check, double-check, and triple check your document. Use spell check and ask a few different people to proof the resume before sending it to employers.

3. **Send the same generic cover letter to every employer.** The cover letter is the perfect opportunity to make a connection with the employer and explain how you can help solve their problems. Don't go vanilla here. Tailor your cover letter to the employer and the position for which you are applying.

4. **Neglect to research the company before the interview.** With so much information on the Internet, there is no excuse for not knowing about the company you are interviewing with. Use Vault (www.vault.com), Glassdoor (www.glassdoor.com), WetFeet (www.wetfeet.com), Jigsaw (www.jigsaw.com), and LinkedIn (www.linkedin.com) to unearth important information

about the companies and people you are interviewing with and don't forget to take advantage of the research resources available at many public libraries.

5. **Ask everyone they know for a job.** Unless you want your friends and colleagues to stop returning your calls, don't just ask everyone you know for a job. Instead, ask for information about a company, a person, an industry, etc. Let your contacts know you value their knowledge and insights. Through these exploratory conversations, they may be able to point you in the direction of a possible job opportunity even if they can't help you land that job directly.

6. **Neglect to send a thank you letter following an interview.** It's not just a courtesy. It is an opportunity to make a second impression on the person you just interviewed with and remain top of mind. Send the thank you letter within 24 hours of the interview. A few paragraphs with a thank you and a recap of why you are the perfect match for the job can help keep you on the hiring manager's short list.

7. **Fail to leverage their network.** Some people feel that reaching out to their network for contacts means asking for favors. It doesn't. See #5.

8. **Snub social media.** Social media allows you to be in multiple places at the same time. It is a great way to build efficiencies into your search strategy. It's time to embrace social media rather than turning your nose up at it.

9. **Complain.** It's easy to blame the company or the economy for your job search frustrations. But it won't get you a job any faster. Find a few close confidents you can vent to and don't spread your frustration to others. Keep a journal to help you chronicle your search journey and help get your feelings out.

10. **Give up.** This is perhaps the scariest one of all. Many people have given up. Unemployment benefits won't last forever. At some point, you will have to get back in the game. If you have dropped out of the race for several months, getting back in is much harder. Keep at it. Plan job search activities every day. You will be scheduling meetings with friends and colleagues, doing Internet research, building your online network, working on your resume, practicing your elevator pitch, etc. There is much to do. Job searching is a full-time job. Now's not the time to take a vacation.

Barbara Safani

How to Protect Your Career if a Tornado Hits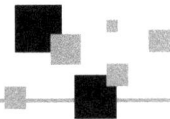

One year a tornado ripped through my hometown in Queens, New York. New Yorkers aren't exactly used to tornadoes and the event really took us by surprise. Many of my friends posted pictures of the damage and one friend shared a picture of a weeping willow tree that had been broken in two by the storm. This was perhaps the most moving image from the storm. There are many majestic weeping willow trees in front of various apartment buildings in Queens. Many of these trees are well over a hundred years old and I have fond memories of climbing them as a kid. It's the type of tree that you assume can withstand anything and will be there forever.

The damaged weeping willow tree reminded me of the economic conditions of late 2008. Lehman Brothers and Merrill Lynch were a lot like that tree. They were old, established firms and for years, they seemed invincible. But they weren't. Their demise was like a tornado and the devastation was palatable. Overnight, people who thought their jobs were secure had no job to speak of. What happened at Lehman Brothers and Merrill Lynch had a ripple effect on the rest of the economy, and many are still feeling that impact years later.

No job is ever really safe. Skies can be sunny one moment and pitch black the next. Being prepared for a change in the weather and a change at a company is important. Would you be prepared for a career tornado? Here are a few things to consider doing before the dark clouds set in.

1. **Update your resume.** Even if you are happy in your current job and feel safe, it never hurts to have a current resume. With an up-to-date resume you will always be prepared should a new opportunity present itself. To get the process started, think introspectively about what you have accomplished since you last wrote your resume. Try to think of accomplishments in terms of how you did things smarter, faster, or more efficiently and how you've helped the organizations you've supported make money, save money, save time, eliminate redundancies, grow the business, or keep the business.

2. **Keep networking.** People always ask me how long it will take them to find a new job. I generally tell them that the length of their search is frequently correlated to the quality of their network at the time they begin looking. People with strong networks always know people who are thinking about them for other opportunities. Even if you are comfortable in your current job, continue to find ways to be active in professional communities or volunteer your knowledge or time to help others. Building visibility and credibility now will help you weather the storm if the situation in your company changes suddenly down the road.

3. **Keep learning.** It's easy to sit back and think you have all the necessary skills and training to do your job. But if you had to change jobs, would the depth and breadth of your knowledge be strong enough to position you for other opportunities? It's wise to think ahead and figure out ways to stay on the leading edge of your profession so you never become obsolete.

Like the weather, there are many aspects of our careers that we can't control. But by concentrating on the things we can control, we increase the chances of landing a new job quickly if our current job takes an unexpected turn for the worse.

Job Seekers: You Are Fooling Yourself If...

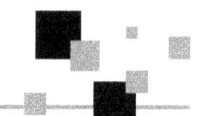

1. **You are expecting to get calls for interviews because you posted your resume online.** Despite all the advice and statistics to the contrary, job seekers continue to spend most of their job search time posting on job boards. It's fine to apply for positions that you are truly qualified for online. However, it is imperative that you create alternative plans for getting your foot in the door at those employers. Talk to recruiters, find someone in your network that may know someone at the company, or use tools such as LinkedIn or Jigsaw to find a potential decision maker at that company. Posting on the job boards with thousands of other applicants will rarely get you noticed.

2. **You think keywords in resumes are "nice to have."** More and more recruiters and hiring managers are using applicant tracking systems to source candidates, and they may never find you if your resume doesn't contain relevant keywords. Stop debating the importance of keywords and start putting them in your resume. Applicant tracking systems are getting more sophisticated and they are here to stay.

3. **You think the format and presentation of your resume is inconsequential.** I often write posts about the importance of what I call "resume bling," the use of visuals such as graphs and charts and, in some cases, color or images to show impact or differentiate oneself from the pack. This idea continues to scare people who think this isn't proper resume etiquette because it will make their resume look different. Sorry, but looking different is the point.

4. **You think networking is just brown nosing.** I get these comments about networking all the time and even hear from people who say they would never "stoop" to try to build relationships with people as part of their job search. They are missing the boat on the concept of giving to give and being authentic. People want to do business with people they know. Take a general interest in people, always, and they will be there to help you when you need an introduction.

5. **You think online networking is not necessary for you.** Sometimes my senior level clients tell me they are very well known in their professional circles, so LinkedIn is not necessary for them. They may be well known, but many hiring managers and recruiters expect to see a consistent online representation of who you are professionally.

Take a long hard look at your search strategy. Are you making progress or just fooling yourself?

Making the Job Search Fun

How can you overcome the negative aspects of the job search and stay upbeat if your search efforts haven't landed you a job yet? Job searching is tough and it's certainly a lot of work, but it doesn't have to be drudgery. Here are suggestions for things you can do to make the job search more rewarding, more enlightening, and hopefully more fun.

Eat. No, I'm not talking about pity eating and downing a bag of chips and a pint of ice cream in front of the TV. Meeting a friend for coffee, a drink, or lunch is a great way to combine something pleasant and fun with some power networking.

Write. Journaling is a great way to record how you are feeling during your search and examine the trends that could be indicators of what is working in your search and what is not. Some even turn their journals into blogs to create a following and make new friends and contacts as they chronicle their unemployment experience.

Study. Did you know that the Department of Labor funds job training programs? You may qualify for training in a specific skill or funding to return to school to complete a degree program. Going back to school can be fun.

Exercise. Aerobic conditioning and weight workouts can help you feel better and burn calories more efficiently during the day. Pilates can help reduce the muscle aches often associated with hours of sitting at a desk hunched over a computer, and many people find that a regular yoga practice is a great way to reduce stress.

Primp and Pamper. This is not an indulgence. The little details like your hair and nails count during a job search. It can also be rejuvenating to get a new hairstyle or experiment with a new nail color.

Shop. I'm not suggesting a totally new wardrobe, but a new scarf, tie, hair clip, or handkerchief can change up the interview suit you are tired of wearing and give you a renewed sense of confidence.

Read. Books by Harvey Mackay and Keith Ferrazi have provided inspiration for millions of job seekers over the years. Check out some of their titles at your local library.

Reconnect. Get over your concerns about reconnecting with past colleagues and friends. Social media tools like LinkedIn and Facebook have made it fun, easy (and less creepy) to get back in touch with people from your past. Rekindle past relationships and you are bound to find a friend or two that can help you with some aspect of your search.

Let the Job Search Begin!

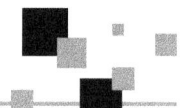

Olympic athletes often describe how the mental preparation for their sport is as important as the physical preparation. They use mental techniques to set goals, stay on target, and envision their success. What if job seekers could adopt this Olympic-winner attitude and create internal "tapes" to motivate them and move past their challenges? Perhaps then the setbacks they face would seem manageable and the hope would stay alive. Here are some positive messages job seekers should be sending themselves on a regular basis.

1. I will maintain a healthy life style so I can manage my search at an optimal performance level.

2. I will challenge myself to reach out to new people who may be able to help me with my search.

3. I will accept the help of friends and family during this difficult time even if it makes me a bit uncomfortable.

4. I will seek out coaches and mentors who can help me move closer to my goal.

5. I will put in the time necessary to research potential employers and market myself directly to them.

6. I will examine my resume and other personal marketing collateral to make sure they are the best they can be.

7. I will celebrate the victory of landing an interview, even if I don't ultimately get the job.

8. I will not blame external factors for my situation.

9. I will be a good team member and support others in their job search when I can.

10. I will regularly envision the end goal of landing my new job.

Some days it's hard for an athlete to muster up the motivation for the grueling training session ahead of him. Likewise, some days it's hard for a job seeker to stay motivated in a challenging market. Positive self-talk can help. So does keeping your eye on the gold. Let the games begin!

5 Things Not to Say to a Job Seeker During the Holiday Season

Everyone wants to help a friend in need, especially during the holiday season where depression over a job search can be at an all time high. If you have a friend who is currently job searching, the natural tendency is to try more diligently to help him during this time of year. But before you start dishing out advice, make sure it's actually helpful. Consider these typical comments/suggestions that many well-meaning friends make during someone's job search. Are you really helping or is there a better tact you could take to support your friend?

1. **I'm sure things will pick up in the New Year.** This is a cop out on your part and just a way to make the conversation an easier one for you. Show some genuine empathy and let your friend know that you understand that the holidays can be a difficult time to be in a job search and that you are there for him and are willing to offer emotional support.

2. **It's brutal out there; I have another friend who has been out of work for 18 months.** Perhaps you are trying to make your friend feel better by showing him he is not alone in his struggles. But comparing two people's job searches is like comparing apples and oranges. So many factors, including the person's profession, industry, geography, years of

experience, resume, quality of their network, and general search strategy can influence the length of the search. Rather than focus on what you think is the norm for a job search, concentrate on ways you can help your friend accelerate theirs. Invite him to events or social functions where you think he may be able to meet people to expand his network or offer to introduce him to one of your colleagues.

3. **Let me take a look at your resume; maybe I can offer some suggestions.** Unless you screen or write resumes on a regular basis, don't offer to critique someone else's. What you think looks professional may not be what hiring authorities, recruiters, and applicant tracking softwares are looking for. Refer your friend to a professional resume writer instead.

4. **Have you posted your resume on any job boards? I hear a lot of people are using (insert job board here).** Believe me, most job seekers have already explored this option with minimal results. Hearing the suggestion from you is like rubbing salt into a wound. Rather than recommending he show up at a job board party with thousands of other applicants, offer him an introduction to someone in your network.

5. **Maybe you should start your own business. You've always been good at (fill in the blank).** While your suggestion has good intentions, your friend might not be ready to wrap their head around the concept of starting their own business. In addition, he might not really be cut out for it. Starting a business requires an enormous amount of thought, time, energy, and introspection. It is generally not an ideal short-term solution to a job loss.

If you have a friend who is in a job search during the holiday season, offer him a meal, an ear, an introduction, and your time. He will get much more mileage out of that kind of support than he will from often misplaced suggestions for what he should be doing. Don't focus on the quick fix solution; instead, focus on supporting him and being there for him.

10 Things To Do Before the Pink Slip Arrives

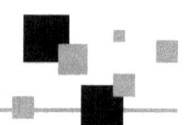

Here are 10 things everyone should do now, just in case a pink slip arrives in the future. Even if you think your job is secure, these tips are part of any successful, ongoing career management strategy.

1. **Audit Your Resume.** Most people's resumes read like job descriptions with little or no evidence of the person's impact on the organizations they supported. Review your resume to see if your document reads like a laundry list of job tasks or an accomplishment-focused, metrics-driven self-marketing tool. If your document screams vanilla, consider rewriting your resume or hiring a professional resume writer to help you.

2. **Gather Testimonials.** When someone considers you for an interview, you are basically a risk. The entire interview process is really an exercise in mitigating that risk. The hiring manager is trying to determine if you really have the skills and experience you have chronicled on your resume. A great strategy for gaining the confidence of the hiring manager is to prove your value to an employer through supervisor, client, and vendor testimonials. These quotes may be added to your resume or showcased through the endorsements feature on networking and identity management sites such as LinkedIn or Naymz (www.naymz.com). This type of 360-degree feedback can help you achieve greater credibility with hiring authorities and improve your chances of being hired.

3. **Reconnect.** Map out all the relationships that you have fostered throughout your life and think of authentic ways to reconnect with those you may have lost touch with over the years. Facebook and Classmates are great tools for reconnecting with people you went to school with and LinkedIn makes it easy to reconnect with former colleagues.

4. **Do a Favor for Someone.** Maybe you have a friend that needs assistance with a home improvement project or some help watching their kids for a few hours while they run some important errands. Think of ways to help others. This makes you more top of mind with them should you need their help in the future.

5. **Join a Professional Association.** So many people ignore the benefits of being part of a professional organization and only join once they are in a job search. Since relationships in these circles may take time to build, it is much better to join and give back to your professional community before you start asking for information or job leads.

6. **Volunteer.** Become visible in communities that are important to you. Perhaps that is the PTA at your child's school, the co-op board in your apartment building, or the local animal shelter. Help others and they are more likely to reciprocate.

7. **Get a Flu Shot.** Better yet, get a full check up and have your teeth cleaned as well. If you find yourself in a job search, you want to remain healthy and you also want to have these expenses covered while you can still take advantage of your company's health insurance benefits.

8. **Manage Your Finances.** Do you know what you would do with your 401K or other investments if you lost your job tomorrow? Read up on your options or find a financial advisor to help you.

9. **Avoid Toxic People.** Stay away from people who are chronic complainers, repeatedly report on how much money they have lost, or continuously quote unemployment statistics. Instead, find a buddy who can offer support, advice and friendship and possibly make important introductions and share job leads.

10. **Spend Time With Your Family.** Your family can provide tremendous comfort during stressful times. Eat meals together, read to your kids, and have some alone time with your spouse. Doing so can help relieve some of the tension you may be feeling and remind you of all the ways you are blessed.

Email Etiquette During a Job Search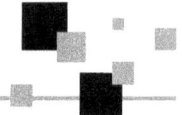

I once heard a story about someone who quit their job over the content of an email. Through conversation and a few apologies, the employee returned to work, but when you think about it, it is amazing how powerful email can be. A misuse of capital letters, a penchant for constantly hitting "send to all," and endless disclaimers, inspirational messages, and graphics on emails can put some people over the edge. Email plays an important role in a job search, but it's got to be managed properly. Here are a few tips for using email in a search campaign.

1. **When sending resumes and follow up letters, always use a compelling subject line.** Don't just type in John Smith's resume...instead try Award Winning Creative Director or Bi-lingual Marketing Executive. Stand out from the crowd and show a glimpse of your professional identity and personal brand.

2. **Always use a signature line.** Make it easy for your contacts to get in touch with you. Include a brief signature line with your name, phone, and email address...every time you send an email. In addition to being a courtesy to your reader, the signature line also creates a more professional presentation.

3. **When following up on job leads, don't send multiple emails.** One email is enough. Supplement your follow up efforts with phone calls, but don't leave multiple messages. Leave one message and then call different times of the day and different days of the week in an attempt to get the person live.

4. **Realize when a conversation is better.** If you find yourself going back and forth more than two times on the same question or issue with a potential hiring manager or recruiter, it's probably time for a phone call.

Is Age Really What's Holding You Back?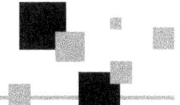

Older job seekers frequently worry about being eliminated from an employer's consideration because of their age. While I'm not denying that ageism exists, I think the real issue that hurts an older job seeker's chances is relevance. If an older worker can't prove that they have kept up with technology and leading-edge concepts for their industry or job function, they will lose out to their younger counterparts that appear more "in the know." So how do you counter potential age bias and quickly show hiring managers that you are just as relevant as the next applicant? Here are a few suggestions.

1. **Add your LinkedIn url to your resume and create a LinkedIn strategy.** Placing your LinkedIn url alongside your contact information on your resume shows employers you are using LinkedIn to network and be found. Adding the url to your business card is a great way to say, "here's my resume" without actually handing someone a copy. Including the url gives the contact the option of learning more about you online. Check out the book I'm on LinkedIn...Now What??? to learn how to leverage LinkedIn for job searching.

2. **Get on Twitter and start having relevant online conversations with opinion leaders in your industry.** Acknowledging the power of Twitter and becoming an active user can help accelerate your job search and get you on the radar of decision makers in your industry. Spend a little bit of time lurking to see how others are using the tool and then jump in. To learn more about how Twitter can help you in your job search check out the book The Twitter Job Search Guide.

3. **Attend a Tweet up or a Meet Up.** Tweet Ups are live meetings where people who have connected on Twitter can meet in person. Meet Up is a site where you can find people in your geography who are interested in the

same topics as you (both professional and personal) to arrange meeting in person in a group setting.

4. **Take the time to learn something new.** If you've been a writer or editor for a traditional publication, learn how to use blogging software. If you are a mainframe computer specialist, learn a new technology. If you are a PR professional, learn how to manage social media communities to engage your audience. You get my drift. Figure out what is leading-edge for your industry and learn how to do it.

5. **Lose phrases like "back in the day."** You will quickly turn off recruiters and hiring managers if you spend too much time focusing on what worked in the past. Back in the day, my mom could "take a letter" like nobody's business and push the return bar on her manual typewriter with speed and agility. But that's not really relevant in today's world, so why waste precious space on a resume or time during an interview referencing it?

6 Common Job Search Mistakes

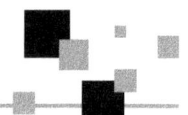

A job search is like a journey and sometimes it's easy to take a wrong turn and neglect some of the important strategies that contribute to a productive and efficient search. Below are some of the most common mistakes I see among job seekers and some tips for getting your search back on track.

Mistake #1: You don't have an accomplishment-focused resume. Job seekers often create resumes that are no more than a laundry list of job tasks. Such documents do little to differentiate you from the competition. Instead of writing about things you did, write about the accomplishment within the task. Rather than saying that you make widgets, explain that you exceeded the company's quota for making widgets by 25% by retooling the production process and eliminating redundancies.

Mistake #2: You have neglected your network. If you don't stay in touch with friends, acquaintances, colleagues, and clients, your request to reconnect with them after the relationship has been dormant for so long will be met with suspicion. If you only reach out to your network when you need a favor, your network will dry up very quickly. Find ways to remain involved in the lives of your acquaintances, colleagues, and clients and plan to give more than you get. Create natural touch points for staying connected. Send articles that you think might be of interest to your network or create a personalized e-card to recognize someone's birthday. Invite people for coffee and attend events at professional associations.

Mistake #3: You don't have an online presence. Your resume says you are an accomplished professional and a leader in your field. Yet when a hiring manager or recruiter puts your name in a search engine, nothing comes up or they find others with the same name and can't distinguish you from the others they see listed. Many hiring authorities will want to research your candidacy past the resume and an online search is one of the best ways to do this. Make it easy for them to find you by creating customized online identity, business, and social networking profiles. Some important tools to consider using are LinkedIn, ZoomInfo (www.zoominfo.com), and Google+ (https://plus.google.com).

Mistake #4: You don't have a personal marketing plan. Think about what you want in your next job. Identify the type of position, industry and companies, geography, company size and corporate culture you are interested in. Then do some research to uncover which organizations best match the descriptions of your dream companies and market yourself directly to those companies, whether they have an open position or not. Reach out to your network to see if you are connected to someone who knows someone in that company and ask for an introduction. The goal is to build inroads into these companies before they need you and later leverage that relationship when they are in need of new talent.

Mistake #5: You don't have a system for organizing and tracking your job search materials. When you are in a job search, you start to accumulate a lot of information. You may have different versions of your resumes, multiple cover letters, scores of job postings you have applied to, business cards from networking contacts, company research, and job search articles and tips. You need a spreadsheet or CRM system for organizing and automating this information as much as possible so you can quickly retrieve what you need and cut down on the clutter.

Mistake #6: You don't have an accountability partner. Being in a job search is often like being on a roller coaster. There are highs and lows, and job seekers need to have someone in their lives to help them move forward and remain accountable for their search. Relying on a friend or loved one for support can sometimes be problematic and add stress to the relationship. A better strategy is to find someone else in a job search and partner with that person to share advice and leads and offer support.

5 Ways to Lose Your Job in the Electronic Age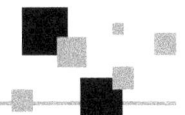

By now you know that displaying pictures of you partying on Facebook or tweeting about how much you hate your boss are electronic no no's. There are other, less well known mistakes that people are making every day at work that can get them and their employers in hot water. Here are five of them.

1. Textual Harassment. Thinking about texting a co-worker on your company cell phone to ask if they want to go for a drink after work? Think again. If your advances are unwanted, you could be accused of textual harassment and the accuser will have the electronic breadcrumbs to back up their claim.

2. Privacy Breaches. Want to shoot your boss an email to let him know that a colleague won't be in today because she is going to the doctor for chemotherapy or a colonoscopy? Don't do it. HIPPA legislation was enacted to ensure that people are protected against having their health information exposed electronically.

3. Emailing While Off Duty. Are some of your employees non-exempt workers who are paid an hourly rate and are eligible for overtime pay? If so, your company may have a strict policy against them doing company work remotely on a company laptop or cell phone after hours.

4. Blogging Without a Disclaimer. Pondering starting a blog to express your musings about life at a particular company? Check to see if your company has a social media policy. Many companies will either request that you don't mention your affiliation with the company on your personal blog or that you add a disclaimer stating that the views expressed on the blog are yours alone and not reflective of the company's position.

5. Electronic Organizing. Union organizers are using electronic leafleting to encourage employees in non-union shops to print and sign authorization cards and distribute union literature. Many organizers have been able to fly under the radar of companies with these methods because they are not as invasive as traditional union activity, but before you forward that email to your co-workers, find out if your company has a clearly defined policy against this type of activity. Going against the company policy could land you on probation or cost you your job.

Is Your Name Hurting Your Chances of Landing a Job?

My son has a name that is very common in some parts of the world but not very common in the United States. When you hear a person's name, do certain thoughts and associations come to mind? I started thinking about how birth names might affect a job seeker's candidacy and wondering if they can actually play a role in the hiring process or lead to discrimination. Here are three situations where I think, in some cases, a job seeker's name could potentially influence the hiring decision.

Names associated with a generation

I recently read a list of the top baby names for the last decade. Some of the names for girls that made the list this decade were Madison, Cheyenne, Sydney, Destiny, Makayla, and Brianna. Forget about finding names like Karen, Donna, Debra, and Barbara high up on the list. They are the names of generations past. It makes you wonder if hiring managers will try to peg the age of a candidate once they hear their name and if their decision to bring that person in for an interview could be influenced by this.

Ethnic sounding names

Names that have come to be associated with another culture or are hard for some to pronounce may be scrutinized more than those that are more mainstream American. I've had clients tell me they "Americanize" their name on their resumes to avoid this. Remember all the media around President Obama's middle name Hussein? Is it possible that candidates are being judged on their names on a regular basis and this affects their ability to land the interview?

Names shared by multiple people

In this Internet age, more and more hiring managers are surfing the web, typing the names of applicants into search engines and reviewing the results before they even call the applicant in for an interview. But what if your name is Fred Smith or Mary Jones? How many pages of results will the hiring manager need to sift through before finding the right one? Will they have the patience to do this or will it just be easier to move on to another candidate?

I'm certainly not recommending that anyone change their name, but I think the nuances of a name are important to pay attention to during a job search. If you have a difficult-to-pronounce name, you can try including your American nickname in parenthesis on your resume or just use an abbreviated form of your given name. If you have a common name, you can use your middle name to further differentiate you from all the other people who share your name. And if you think your name somewhat "dates" you, try to include content in your resume that proves that your skills are relevant in the current economy.

Obviously, we are more than our names and we want to presume that hiring managers have good intent when screening applicants. But it doesn't hurt to ask ourselves, "What's in a name?"

How Many Americans Are Happy at Work?

According to a 2011 Mercer survey of close to 2,400 US employees, half of US employees are not happy in their jobs. Here are some other interesting stats from the survey:

- 32% of US workers are currently considering leaving their organization, up from 23% in 2005.

- 21% are not looking to leave but view their employers unfavorably and have low scores on key measures of engagement.

- Only 43% of US employees believe they are doing enough to financially prepare for retirement – down from 47% in 2005, and just 41% believe their employers are doing enough to help them prepare, up slightly from 38%.

- 68% of employees rate their overall benefits program as good or very good, down from 76% in 2005, while 59% say they are satisfied with their health care benefits, down from 66%.

- US workers show lower satisfaction with base pay (53% satisfied, down from 58% in 2005).

- 42% of employees believe promotions go to the most qualified employees in their organization, up from 29% in 2005, and 46% agree that their organization does an adequate job of matching pay to performance, up from 33%.

- The youngest workers are most likely to leave their companies – 40% of employees age 25–34 and 44% of employees 24 and younger.

Which half are you in at work? The happy half or the unhappy half?

Would You Marry Someone Who Was Unemployed?

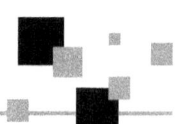

According to a recent survey conducted by YourTango and ForbesWomen, 75% of women surveyed said they would not marry someone without a job and 65% said they wouldn't get married if they were the one who was unemployed. But 91% of single women said they would marry for love over money. Huh? Some of the other survey stats intrigued me as well including:

- 55% of women would give up their careers to take care of children if their partners asked them to but only 28% would ask the same of their partner.

- 77% of women believe they can simultaneously have a fulfilling relationship and family life, as well as a successful career yet only 43% said their work/life balance is what they would like it to be.

- 62% of women in a relationship said they only spend three waking hours with their partner during the work week.

- 42% of women said that if they had an extra hour each day, they would spend it alone rather than with their partners, friends, or family.

Is it possible that women have been conditioned to want love over money, but the prospect of being with someone who is unemployed challenges a need for stability? Is there a biological predisposition for women to assume the man will be the primary breadwinner?

What about the work/life balance issue? Is it conceivable that women have been told for so long that they can have it all that they naturally believe this is so, even when their lives don't reflect any such work/life balance? Do woman want it all and then decide to "chuck it" once kids come into the picture and there is an opportunity to raise a family full-time?

I don't have the answers to any of these questions, but I think the survey represents the state of flux, turmoil, and confusion that many women feel. We want it all, but having it all simultaneously seems to be mathematically impossible. Maybe there just aren't enough hours in the day to have it all at the same time. Are there other options? What do you think?

Changing Careers: Look Before You Leap

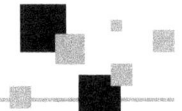

I frequently talk to people who want to change careers. They often tell me one of these four things:

- I hate my job.
- I don't think my job is a good fit.
- I want to do something more meaningful.
- My friends tell me I would make a great (fill in the blank)

When I hear these statements, I'm not always convinced that the person expressing these doubts really wants to change careers. Instead, I often believe that there is something else going on at work or in the person's personal life, which is causing the unrest or thoughts of quitting, and it's important to explore these factors before jumping into a career change.

Career change can be challenging on many fronts. Landing a job in a new career generally takes more time than landing one in a linear career path. You will need a robust network of contacts and many, many advocates to get your foot in the door. A career change may require significant education costs and there is no guarantee that acquiring that education will lead to a new job. The most logical career changes are those that have a recognizable intersection between the old and new careers such as a sales person going into marketing or an operations professional switching to human resources.

In over 75% of the cases where I coach clients considering a career change, after in-depth discussion, introspection, and assessment, it is frequently determined that the client doesn't hate what they do; they hate the person they work for. Study after study shows that people don't leave companies; they leave bad bosses. So before you embark on a full-blown career change, ask yourself the following questions:

1. What tasks that are part of my job do I enjoy doing?
2. What tasks that are part of my job do I hate doing?
3. Am I good at what I do? Have others commented on my strengths?
4. What types of tasks do I want to do that are not part of my current job? Is there an opportunity to do these tasks in the future as part of my job?
5. What types of situations in my current job stress me out?
6. How much does my relationship with my boss affect my feelings towards my job?
7. Do my feelings about the company culture affect my feelings about my job?
8. Can I remember a time when I did similar work and enjoyed what I was doing?
9. Are there growth opportunities for me or is my industry/ job function contracting?
10. Am I willing to put in the time and effort necessary to change careers?
11. Have I considered the financial ramifications of changing careers?
12. Am I willing to take a step (or two) backwards to achieve my new career goals?
13. What would my perfect job look like and is this a realistic expectation?

14. What are my priorities? How important are money, time off, meaningful work, or the goals of the organization to me?

Answering these questions may help you gain clarity around your reasons for embarking on a career change. Your answers may help you sort out what you can and cannot live with. Armed with this information you may decide that a retooling of your current career is more prudent than a total career change. On the other hand, your responses may validate that a career change is in fact the right path to take.

People change careers every day, but it's always advisable to make sure you are changing careers for the right strategic long-term reasons and not making a decision based solely on your emotions. Look before you leap and find others to support you in your journey.

Career Advice from My Dad

While my dad was never a career counselor and never even had to face a career transition (he was with one company for 30 years), he did give me some sage advice about my career along the way. Here are a few of my favorite nuggets:

You won't always get along with your boss.

Everyone I've ever met has an interesting story about a bad boss. The trick is to figure out either how to manage that relationship or get out of it. The DISC assessment tool is very useful for figuring out how you communicate with people and how those around you respond to your method of communication. It can help you discover how to tweak your communication style to improve your relationship with a difficult boss.

You will never be able to please everyone.

It seems like our entire lives are spent trying to please someone - a teacher, a boss, a family member. Some people only hear from their bosses when something goes wrong. Be sure to keep track of your stories of success throughout the year so your discussion at performance review time focuses on your positive contributions rather than just the things that need to be improved.

No job is worth risking your health.

I meet many people who have sacrificed their health for their jobs. Stress can contribute to numerous health issues including obesity, heart disease, and depression. Examine your career choices and regularly assess how well they align with your overall life goals.

Getting fired is not the worst thing that can happen in life.

Being fired can be an enormous blow to one's ego, but many people report that it was the best thing that ever happened to them because it allowed them to gain perspective on a bad situation, discover their strengths, and move forward to a more fulfilling career.

Don't expect others to manage your career.

My dad taught me a long time ago that no one cares about my career as much as I do. It's certainly beneficial to have a mentor along the way, but ultimately you have to own your career. Take responsibility for that ownership by keeping your resume up to date, networking regularly, maintaining relationships with recruiters, and monitoring your online identity.

The Future of the Job Search

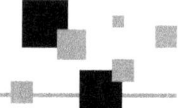

What will the world of job search and work be like when the next generation of workers (sometimes called Generation Z) ventures out in search of their first job in the next decade? I've been observing how integral technology is to a teen's everyday life and trying to make predictions for how technology will affect the job search process and the way employers market themselves to candidates.

Here are my observations on 10 electronic influencers and my predictions for how they will continue to change job searching as we know it.

1. Google

Whenever I ask my kids a question about something or someone, they immediately go online to find the answer. Want to know a movie star's age? Google him or her and you will quickly find it on IMDb. Need to know where the nearest Starbucks is? Hop onto Mapquest. So it seems pretty logical that by the time my kids begin their first job search, their online presence will be checked out by every decision-maker. Everyone will have an online identity and everyone will need to take their online identity seriously.

2. Multiple Instant Messaging Platforms

You think you are hip because you have synched your Facebook and Twitter status updates? Most teens are on Facebook, 10+ IM screens, a video chat, and their electronic account for school assignments. They may also be playing a video game while simultaneously listening to iTunes, watching TV and possibly even doing their homework. They are tapped into multiple communities, participating fully in all of them, and still finding time for themselves! Tomorrow's employee won't work in a linear fashion. They will need to work on projects concurrently while incorporating feedback from colleagues. Their process may look different from generations past, but they will get the job done.

3. Information Banks

When I was a kid, you got a little notepad at the beginning of the year to write down your homework assignments. Today, kids can retrieve their homework assignments from a number of sources including a school website, teacher blog, a moodle (a tool used to augment face-to-face learning and foster discussion), or from general emails from their teachers. Moreover, they are expected to monitor all modes of communication at all times. My prediction is that tomorrow's job-seeker will easily assimilate information from many different sources and will combine all possible resources to find quality information related to their job search. They won't become frustrated by the information overload that most of us feel when dealing with constant emails, status updates, etc. They will figure out ways to pay attention to all incoming information and filter out unnecessary or redundant messages.

4. Texting

From my observations, kids don't spend that much time on the phone. If they are on the phone, it's to berate their friend or parent for not responding to their text message. Most kids view texting as a much faster method of communication and will chose text over a phone call any day. So one could draw the conclusion that more and more job opportunities will be pitched via text messages and I will be so bold as to predict that rejection letters will come in the form of text messages as well. That may sound cold to us, but I don't think tomorrow's job seeker will see it that way, and they might even prefer that to a phone call. No scientific evidence here -- just a hunch.

5. Email

Job seekers often ask me if it is better to send a typed or handwritten thank you note and if it should be emailed or sent by snail mail? I think that question finally will be put to rest with the next generation of job seekers. Many kids can barely write in cursive. They learned it in the third grade and never used it, because since that time, they typed assignments on a computer. It looks like script is going the way of cuneiform and emails and texts will be the only accepted form for a thank you letter. And as for snail mail, I can count the number of times my kids have mailed a letter on one hand, so I really doubt that tradition is going to be around for much longer.

6. Social Networking

I have to believe that by the time Gen Z enters the world of work, all of a company's employees will be connected via some sort of electronic networking platform. But they won't only be used for idle banter. Instead, they will be used to create work teams, work collaboratively on projects, and build consensus. Kids already are using social networking platforms and video chat to work on school projects and study for tests. Using these same tools for work seems like a natural progression.

7. Reality TV

Is there any other kind of TV anymore? With reality TV, everything is a test, a challenge, a comparison to others. There is a lot of subjectivity in the process and the outcome is not always fair. Hmm. Sounds a lot like interviewing. And maybe interview practices will begin to mirror reality TV. Want to interview 10 people for a position? Why not bring them in at the same time and give them job-specific tasks to complete independently and as part of a team? What better way to determine how they will fit in with a company's corporate culture?

8. Computer Simulations

The Sims, a popular teen computer game, simulates life situations and the objective of the game is to organize the characters' lives to help them reach their personal goals. Guitar Hero puts the player in the role of rock star and World of Warcraft lets players combat each other, fight monsters, or complete quests. Companies such as Deloitte & Touche already are using simulations to teach kids how to solve the types of problems that accountants face and to get kids interested in the field. I predict that more companies will create simulation tools so that candidates can truly experience a day in the life of an employee at their company. Perhaps such simulations will help weed out inappropriate candidates and streamline the hiring process. It could happen.

9. Video Chat

As I mentioned earlier, video chat is a big part of the communications circle for many teens. As these kids start interviewing for positions down the road, video interviews probably will become more mainstream as well.

10. The Wild Card

There's probably some other technology on the horizon that will greatly influence job searching in the years to come. Maybe it's a leading-edge resume parsing tool, a new online community that revolutionizes the way job seekers connect with decision makers, or a humanoid robot programmed to ask and record candidate responses to interview questions. Who knows?

Barbara Safani

Top Career Mistakes Boomers Make Online

To a job seeker, the Internet can sometimes seem like the wild, wild West. It often seems like there is danger at every turn. Job search scams are on the rise and there have been many reported cases of people having their online profiles hacked with detrimental consequences. From what I see, the boomers are often the most cautious about sharing information online; as a Boomer, I understand their concerns.

However, leveraging the power of the Internet and using it intelligently to create visibility for yourself to better manage your career is critical. Below are some of the mistakes I see Boomers making when managing their online identity and reputation.

1. Thinking no news is good news.

Some Boomers believe they don't need to pay attention to their online identity because there is no negative information about them online. But if a hiring manager searches for you online and can't find any information about you that may be viewed negatively as well. Most HR departments now are required to research candidates online, and "over half are making decisions based on positive content they find"; these applicants are missing out on a huge opportunity to make a lasting impression. (source: January 2010 study on online reputation-management by Cross Tab Marketing and Microsoft.)

2. Believing the Internet is a dangerous place.

Privacy tends to be important to Boomers, and the idea of sharing information in an open forum seems unnatural for many. While Boomers are right to be cautious about how much information is shared, there are ways to create an online presence without sharing information that could be collected by others and used in a negative way. Keep full dates of birth off social networking sites and opt for just the day and month instead to protect yourself against potential identity theft. Pay close attention to your privacy settings to make intelligent decisions about what to share and not share with those outside your network.

3. Having a one-dimensional online strategy.

Many Boomers think that the only social networking site they need to pay attention to is LinkedIn. LinkedIn is a must for any professional, but it's not the only way to be found online. Tools that focus on online identity such as Google Profiles and

ZoomInfo help build the number of positive online impressions for you and extend your reach and visibility across the Web.

4. Assuming Facebook is just for kids.

While it's true that Facebook started as a social networking tool for college students, it's come a long way since its launch. Most people find their jobs through people they know -- and since Facebook is based on people you know (more so than LinkedIn), it makes sense to incorporate Facebook into your online social networking strategy. That old friend from high school, or your friend's friend who is in the same profession as you, may be the Facebook "friend" who can put you in touch with the right person for your next job.

5. Feeling that their industry reputation supersedes their online one.

You may have a strong reputation among those who know you, but frequently, when you are looking for a new position, you are reaching out to people who don't know you as well, and you may be competing against others with a more established online presence. It makes sense to cover all bases and build an outstanding online presence to match the one you have created for yourself in your professional niche.

20 Ways to Get a Job

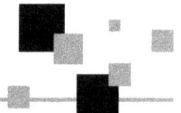

Need some fresh ideas for landing a job? Add these strategies into your mix of job search activities to meet new people, find potential employers and get hired.

1. Go around the gatekeeper.

If you find an open position through a job board or company website, don't only submit your resume to human resources -- they're usually gatekeepers who don't have much control over who ends up getting hired. Instead, go around the gatekeeper and do some Internet research to find the hiring manager or other decision-maker and market your candidacy directly to them.

2. Cybersleuth your way to decision-makers.

Perform keyword searches for companies, job title, etc. on Google and LinkedIn to see if you can find someone in your network connected to the company you want to get into or to request an introduction.

3. Become a stalker (sort of).

Once you find people who are connected to the industries and companies you are interested in, do some research to find out more about them. Do they belong to certain professional associations or do they attend events for certain charities?

4. Tweet. Twitter is a great platform for positioning yourself as a thought leader in your job function and industry. By sharing your ideas with others and allowing your followers to share your thoughts or tweets with their Twitter followers, you can create a powerful presence online and extend your reach exponentially very quickly. The more people who get to know you and understand your area of expertise, the greater the likelihood that they will be able to connect you with someone who can assist in your search.

5. Research industries and job functions that are trending up.

Check out the Occupational Outlook Handbook to learn more about industries and jobs predicted to experience growth over the next decade. The 10 fastest-growing opportunities in recent years were in technology positions for applications such as Twitter, Cloud Computing, iPhone, Facebook. Other positions trending upward were corporate social responsibility expert, blogger, pediatrician, hospitalist, social media expert, and speech language pathologist. Sites such as CareerBuilder and Payscale are also excellent resources for tracking trending industries and job functions.

6. Recognize that the new green movement is somewhat old.

Greentech, Cleantech, and Smart Grid technology are also industries that are trending up, but keep in mind that many traditional industries and job functions are also embracing the green movement and this will facilitate job growth. For example, more and more hotels seek consultants to help them figure out how to make their hotels more eco-friendly, and many companies are consciously measuring their carbon footprint and trying to figure out ways to waste less and recycle more.

7. Think about jobs that can't be outsourced.

Many health care-related jobs including dental assistant, ultrasound technician, paramedic, home care aide, and nurse cannot be outsourced. You may not be trained for one of these careers, but you can certainly try to make inroads with the organizations that employ these professionals -- hospitals, clinics, nursing homes, hospice care, etc. -- as a way to get a foothold in an industry that appears to be at less risk for being outsourced.

8. Ponder what types of business problems need to be solved.

The financial crisis might have resulted in several lost jobs, but with that comes the opportunity for something new. Expect to see organizations creating greater measures for compliance and stricter auditing procedures, and stricter government control. Does your skill set support any of these needs?

9. Channel your inner Uncle Sam.

One of the fastest-growing sectors is the federal sector. It is the only sector that will continue to fill jobs, regardless of economic conditions.

10. Party on.

Are there certain watering holes in your town where people from certain companies hang out on a Thursday night? Frequent the same places; do a bit of eavesdropping and try to introduce yourself in a fun and non-threatening way. If you can somehow become part of their inner circle, you may be able to connect with someone willing to share internal job leads and information on company movement.

11. Buddy up.

Attend networking events with a colleague or fellow job seeker and create a strategy for how to "work the room" separately for optimal results. At the end of the event, share information and compare notes. It's like getting two networking meetings for the price of one.

12. Don't diss the library.

The Internet is great for company research, but don't overlook the library resources such as Hoovers, Edgars, association directories, and yes, even the local yellow pages are great sources of information on companies.

13. Chat it up.

Everywhere. At the line on the bank, the bus, at the gym, at your kids' soccer games. You never know whom the person you are talking to is connected to.

14. Share the love.

Volunteer in professional associations, community projects, and causes you are passionate about. By volunteering, you build trust with others and credibility as a person who can get things done. People are more likely to recommend and refer people they know and trust when paid employment opportunities arise.

15. Be part of the conversation.

Find blogs on topics relevant to your industry and profession and contribute to the conversation. Or if you really enjoy writing, start your own blog and create your own following.

16. Throw a party.

Bringing friends together can help you stay top of mind and facilitate conversations about who knows who, and whom you may be able to get a meeting with.

17. Get some PR.

People have been hired after having their job search stories profiled on TV and in print and online. It's not as hard as it sounds. Sign up with a media leads site like HARO (Help a Reporter Out www.helpareporter.com) and you may get on a journalist's radar. Job searching continues to be a hot topic and your story might just catch the eye of someone who is hiring.

18. Go on vacation.

Really. It doesn't have to be an exotic or expensive vacation. The point is to put yourself in a situation where you meet new people. Doing so generates new conversations. Cruises are a great option because many activities are done in a group. But if you are a landlubber, a weekend trip to a bed and breakfast or a yoga retreat will work as well.

19. Get a hobby.

People tend to build affinity with people they share interests with. Book clubs, wine tastings, and knitting clubs can all be great vehicles for creating and extending relationships and creating opportunities to move the conversation past the topic of the hobby into the realm of other topics that might include your job search. Support groups such as Weight Watchers are another great example of affinity groups where the bond is strong and people tend to help people in other aspects of their life.

20. Go back in time.

Some of the strongest affinities may very well be with people you grew up with and went to school with. Social media platforms such as Classmates and Facebook have made it easier (and less awkward) to reconnect with friends from the past. Old friends are often willing and eager to help by sharing information and even possibly give job leads.

10 Ways a Stay-at-Home Mom Can Stay in the Professional Loop

After a child is born, some women make the decision to stop working to become full-time mothers. Play dates take the place of meetings and anxiety about an upcoming presentation is replaced with concern over a stuffy nose. While many moms know they will return to work at some point, few create and organize a plan for re-entry. When they decide to return, many women experience difficulty negotiating a salary consistent with their level of expertise or accounting for their achievements during their career hiatus.

With a little bit of planning, research, and creativity along with a systematic approach to networking, you can continue to maintain your professional persona while being a full-time mom. Your transition back to the world of work will become a more rewarding and less stressful experience.

Networking is the cornerstone of a successful job search campaign. It is an ongoing process of building and maintaining relationships with people who have the expertise you want and need and reciprocating their help with information that is useful to them. As a mom, you are always networking. Mothers swap advice with other moms about schools, babysitters, pediatricians, baby products, etc. We want to buy our products and services from establishments that are recommended by people we trust.

Job seekers share information in a similar way. They approach their contacts for information about a particular industry or company, discuss their skills and business accomplishments and prove how they can add value to an organization. Relationships are built on reciprocity and trust. By solidifying these ties, job seekers gain the opportunity to request introductions into their contacts' inner circles. Each new contact can lead them closer to a new business opportunity. However, it is crucial they never ask a contact to get them a job. This would create stress in the relationship by implying an unrealistic expectation. However, asking for information is reasonable, even flattering.

Below are some tips for expanding your network and staying connected to your business community during your child caring years. Start networking for business opportunities now so you'll have more viable options when you are ready to return to work.

1. The Playground

It's often said that more deals are made on golf courses than at the office. A close second to the golf course may very well be the playground. The same principles of networking and camaraderie work with a small child in tow. It's easy to strike up a conversation at the swings or the sandbox. Bring some toys that work best in groups like jump ropes, balls and bubble fluid and you're bound to have a captive audience of kids and adults in no time. If many of the children in your neighborhood are with caregivers during the week, it still makes sense to build these relationships. Chances are that the nanny's current employer or their friend's employers are people that are connected to others that you might like to know.

2. Group Classes/Sports Teams

By the time your children are three years old, many classes are "drop off" and parents are asked to wait outside the class area. Use that hour to network with the parents in the class. Try to schedule at least one class on the weekend to maximize the opportunity to communicate with a parent directly. As your kids get older, consider becoming the team parent for your child's sports teams. This enables you to have ongoing contact with the parents of the team members and positions you as an effective organizer or leader.

3. Playgroups

Build a core group of moms (and dads) and establish a weekly playdate. You will make special, long lasting bonds with the parents and establish a support system for a future job search.

4. School/Community

When you volunteer for a position in your child's school or your local community, you are broadening your range of contacts since members of these groups represent multiple professional backgrounds. You are afforded the chance to network with people that you might not meet at work or through a professional organization. Volunteering in your school/community allows you to:

- Position yourself as an insider or expert in a particular area

- Gain access to other members of the community that may be useful professional contacts in the future

- Develop new marketable skills that you can apply to your future job search

When you volunteer, chose a leadership role, such as chairperson for an event or member of the school's executive board. These types of opportunities provide you with much greater visibility and decision-making power than you would receive if you just offer to bake cupcakes for the school picnic.

5. E-groups

Consider setting up an e-group with the people you worked with and wish to maintain a future relationship. This will enable you to keep up with the corporate culture and gossip and will position you well should you decide to return to a previous employer in the future.

6. Alumni Organizations

Classmates.com is a free service that manages online school alumni programs where members can reconnect with old friends, receive reunion updates and post messages.

College/University Alumni Associations are a feature on most school websites. If a chapter for your school does not exist in your area, consider starting one.

7. Professional Organizations

Keep up your memberships with professional organizations or join a new one while you are not working. This allows you to stay current on issues that affect your industry. In addition to offering valuable information via the organization's website, newsletter, or trade publication, most host free or low-cost seminars. Make it a point to stay connected with some fellow members and meet some new ones. Consider taking on a leadership role within your professional community. Chair a committee or submit articles for the association newsletter. Much of the work can be done from home and offers a fair amount of flexibility. Chose the activity that meshes with your childcare schedule and follow through on all assignments. These positions increase your credibility and visibility within your professional community.

8. Share your expertise

Teach a class at your local school, library or community center. If you are a nurse, teach infant CPR. If you are an accountant, share some tips for tax time. Contribute an article to a local newspaper or website or publication within your industry. These activities keep your skills sharp and current and help you build your credibility as an expert within your community.

9. Connect others

Introduce contacts that you think could benefit from each other's experiences. Both will remember the introduction and be more likely to share contacts with you when asked.

10. Create a resume

Keep track of all your accomplishments during the years you are taking care of your children and quantify your results whenever possible. Don't assume that your work will not be valued by the business community because it was done on a volunteer basis. Hiring managers look for candidates that can solve their problems and make or save money for their company. For example, if you organized the school's annual fair, write out a statement explaining your role and quantify what you did, such as, "Generated $25,000 in school funds by organizing a community building event for 800 families." Or if you chaired a committee for a professional organization say, "Increased committee visibility by 40% by actively recruiting and marketing special committee presentations and events." Use your volunteer activities as a way to showcase your ability to lead, persuade and organize. Combine these traits with your professional identity and expertise.

As mothers, we spend a great deal of time nurturing our children's passions and developing their unique skills and attributes. We become so immersed in the amazing process of watching our children grow, that we often forget that we still need to plant professional seeds now so that our careers can blossom in the future. Build your network now and you'll enjoy the benefits when you are ready to renew your job search.

The First 100 Days in a New Job

Whether you are a senior executive of a large, well-known company or a recent college grad, your performance in your next job will be watched closely during your first 100 days on the job. If you have recently accepted a new position or hope to land a new position soon, here are some tips for managing those first critical 100 days.

1. **Study up.** You prepared for your interviews by researching the company and understanding their strengths and challenges. Now that you are in the job, use the first 100 days to dig deeper into the company's mission, brand proposition, and reputation in the market. Read everything you can get your hands on that references the company.

2. **Crack the company code.** When you begin a job at a new company, it can sometimes feel like you've just moved to a foreign country. Many companies have their own acronyms, lingo, inside jokes, etc. Try to buddy up with someone who can act as a translator to get you up to speed quickly.

3. **Showcase your strengths.** You talked about your strengths during the interview process and leveraged past stories of success to prove your value-add. Take charge of a project you know you can deliver on and then make sure that you do.

4. **Document your accomplishments.** It's never too early to start documenting job successes. One year from now, when it is time for your performance review, you want to be able to cite your accomplishments throughout the year, including those achieved within those first critical 100 days.

5. **Break bread with colleagues.** A lot of critical information about the company will not be found in annual reports or monthly newsletters. In order to understand the unofficial rules, company politics, and corporate culture, you need to have ongoing conversations with both management and people in the trenches.

6. **Find a mentor.** Connect with someone who is more senior than you are and has significantly longer company tenure than you. A mentor can help you manage your career by putting you in front of the right people and exposing you to the right resources.

7. **Dress the part.** Don't put away your interview suit just yet. Observe the dress code around you; but remember, you may still be scrutinized more closely than your colleagues. Play it safe and always choose an appropriate, but possibly more conservative, style.

5 Questions to Ask Yourself Before Going Back to School for an MBA

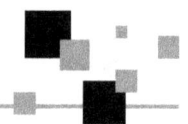

I meet some of my clients after they have completed an MBA program. Some of them have previous work experience in totally unrelated fields and assume that the MBA is an automatic ticket to a new job, a management role, and a higher salary. Often they are very disappointed when they realize that the MBA is not the golden ticket they thought it would be. Before returning to school for an MBA, ask yourself these questions:

Why you are considering the MBA? If you are genuinely interested in the curriculum and your main reason for returning to school is to learn new things, you may be very happy with your decision. If you are doing it because you think you will earn more money, tread carefully. Earning an MBA does not guarantee you will be paid better than your non-MBA counterparts will. They may have gained valuable practical work experience while you were spending your time learning the theories behind management in school.

Does the MBA support the career you have already started or take you in a totally new direction? If the MBA builds on experience you already have in a particular area, gaining the degree may help add an additional level of expertise and relevance. However, if the MBA focus is unrelated to your past experience, just having the MBA won't necessarily open the right doors for you.

Can you get a third party to help pay the tuition costs? If your company offers some tuition reimbursement or if you were previously part of the military, this might be the case. Better to have someone else help defer the costs than end up in debt later on.

How old are you? If you have been working for less than 5 years, getting the MBA may be a logical career move. If you are going back to school after 15+ years, chances are it won't get you as far. The one exception may be an Executive MBA program that your employer is sponsoring.

Are you considering an MBA because you see job postings that say an MBA is preferred? Take this with a grain of salt. The employer may be using this preferred qualification as a screening tool. Networking is still the best way to find a job. Having a relationship and no MBA is generally better than having an MBA and no relationship.

Deciding whether to go back to school is a big decision that requires significant time and money. Regardless of the degree program you are considering, assess how an advanced degree will help position you for future opportunities and be honest with yourself about what a degree can and cannot do. Talk to people who have completed the degree program you are interested in and learn what their outcomes have been. Make an appointment with the school's admissions office to learn about their career resources and support systems, and if possible, their placement rate.

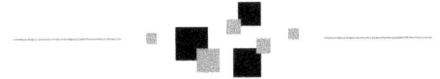

Happy About My Job Search

CHAPTER 2

Is Your Resume a Turkey? Tips for Building More Powerful Resumes and Cover Letters

Frequently, your resume is your first chance to make an impression on a recruiter or hiring manager. You never get a second chance to make a first impression. Therefore, the importance of the resume cannot be underestimated. This chapter offers tips that will help you craft top-notch resumes, cover letters, and thank you letters that get you noticed by hiring managers.

How Long Should My Resume Be?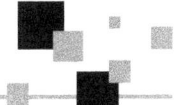

This may just be the most frequent question I am asked regarding resumes. People seem to think that the length of a resume plays a key factor in whether or not the resume is read.

But the reality is that resumes rarely get read, no matter how short or long they are. At least not in their entirety. The length of your resume is not what's most important. What's most important is the quality of the content.

Most hiring managers scan resumes, looking for specific content such as what your profession is, what your skills are, where you have worked (and for how long), your job titles and your educational level. They will be on the lookout for any unexplained employment gaps, excessive job hopping and disjointed career progress.

If the resume passes this initial scan, the hiring manager will look for your accomplishments in past positions and determine how closely aligned these successes are to their organization's future success. If any of this information is difficult to quickly spot on your resume, the reader will probably stop reading very quickly — within seconds.

Some job seekers may be able to package all this information into a one-page resume. Others, particularly those with longer career histories or more frequent job changes, may need two pages. In the U.S. private-sector market, the recommendation is generally not to exceed two pages. If there is something that is truly an important part of your work history, you don't want to have to wait until page three or later to reference it.

So how can you get the best quality information on just one or two pages? Here are some suggestions.

1. **Use space creatively.** Create a resume with margins between .6 and 1.0 on all sides. This gives you flexibility with the way the content is laid out. Place dates of employment in a column on the right-hand margin, rather than the left, to eliminate wasted space. If you need more space on the page for content, consider laying out one of the other sections in a space saving way. For example, instead of centering your contact information at the top of the resume and wasting 5 lines, place your name on the first line and all your contact information in a row on the second line.

2. **Watch your font size.** Font sizes of 10 or 11 generally work best on resumes. Using a smaller font can make the resume difficult to read. But if you need more space, select a font such as Arial or Times New Roman, which both read quite well in 10 point font.

3. **Use bolding to call attention to important information.** Consider placing company names, dates, and job titles in bold so they are easy for the reader to spot. You can also use bold to call out key performance metrics, industry awards and other distinctions.

4. **Edit and then edit again.** Resume writing is a bit different from other forms of writing. Frequently, words such as "a" and "the" can be omitted from the resume because these words are understood by the reader, and the meaning of the message is not compromised by removing them. Read each sentence in your resume and see if there is a way to communicate the same information using fewer words. Frequently in resume writing, less is more.

5. **Think horizontal instead of vertical.** Rather than creating long lists of job skills, language skills, technical competencies, etc., consider placing this information in a horizontal chart to make better use of the space.

6. **Strive for balance.** A one or two page resume can look great. A resume that is one page filled with text and just three lines on a second page looks odd — as if you've run out of things to say. Either prune or expand your content, margins, fonts, and spacing to get your resume down to a full one or two pages.

What are Resume Keywords?

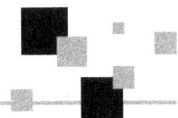

We've all searched for something online by typing in a word or phrase that closely resembles the type of information we are looking for. We find information and make decisions about products and services via these types of searches. Employers use a similar method to find the applicants that best match their open positions. Many companies rely on applicant tracking software to source candidates. By typing certain relevant keywords or phrases into the applicant tracking system, hiring managers can quickly find candidates that fit the requirements for their open positions.

Resume keywords are words used on resumes to describe a competency or skill or to acknowledge experience in a certain job function or industry. If your resume lacks the appropriate keywords, the hiring manager may never find it. Here are some tips for increasing your chances of being found by hiring managers by including appropriate keywords to optimize the compatibility of your candidacy to an employer's needs.

The right keywords

1. One of the best ways to find the keywords that the hiring manager will be searching is to check the job posting or posting for similar jobs. By including those keywords in your resume, you stand a greater chance of being found by the hiring manager.

2. Stem keywords and vary your word choices. For example, rather than just using the word *analyst* on your resume, include variants such as *analysis* or *financial analyst* as well. If you have knowledge of merchandise planning, also include the word *merchandising* or *assortment planning* to the resume to cover your bases.

Also, include different ways of saying certain titles. A CFO should include both *CFO* and *Chief Financial Officer* in the body of the document. A candidate in the pharmaceuticals industry should use both p*harmaceuticals* and *pharma* to describe their industry. A job seeker with experience in mergers and acquisitions should also list the abbreviation M&A, and an HR professional with experience in employment law such as the Family and Medical Leave Act should also use the acronym FMLA. By including variations on the word or phrase, you can increase the likelihood that your resume will be found regardless of the keyword the hiring manager is using for the searching.

3. While it is important to optimize the resume, it must be done in a way that still makes sense to the human reader. Be sure to balance the needs of the human reader with search engine optimization techniques to create the best results. Weave word variations into your document in a logical and natural way.

4. Extend the keyword concept past the resume. Keyword searches are not just limited to applicant tracking tools. Recruiters and hiring managers frequently perform keyword searches on social networking sites such as LinkedIn to find appropriate candidates. Make sure your profile on LinkedIn is robust and includes a lot of keywords.

Keyword suggestions

Below are some examples of how to incorporate keywords into your resume.

CHIEF OPERATING OFFICER (COO)

Operations Risk Mitigation
SEC Registration/Compliance
Acquisitions
Due Diligence
Vendor Selection and Management
Technology Upgrades/Integration
P&L Management
Forecasting/Budgeting
Human Resources
Administration
Hedge Fund
Product Marketing
Investor Reporting
Client Relationship Management
Office Openings and Closings

HUMAN RESOURCES GENERALIST

Talent Acquisition
College Recruiting/Internships
Management Development
Employee Handbook Writing
Competitive Benchmarking
New Hire Orientations
Payroll Administration
EEO and I-9 Compliance
COBRA Administration
ERISA Administration

Reductions in Force
Benefits Design/Administration
Policy Writing/Implementation
Applicant Tracking
Budgeting/Forecasting
Corrective Action Plans
Staff Management

SENIOR LEVEL MERCHANDISING EXECUTIVE

Apparel Merchandising
Merchandising Strategy
Production/SKU Planning
Competitor/Market Analysis
Cross Functional Team Building
Product Development/Launch
International Licensing Relations
Vendor Sourcing/Supplier Relations
Product Standardization
Inventory Management
Leadership and Mentoring
Account Relationship Management
Purchasing Negotiations
Costing
Budgeting
Color and Trend Forecasting
Staff Development

How to Fix Your Common Resume Mistakes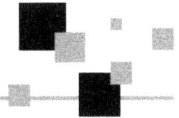

I review a lot of resumes. And most of them have at least one of four major problems related to content, style, and form. Does your resume fall into one or more of these categories? If so, it may be time to perform a checkup on your resume to improve the overall health of your job-search campaign.

1. The job description. These resumes list job responsibilities galore and often look like the writer literally cut and pasted their job description into the resume. What makes a strong resume is not simply the description of your job tasks; it's how successfully you execute on those job tasks that makes you unique and makes you interesting to a hiring manager.

Tip: For each position you have held, create a brief paragraph that describes your job responsibilities and job scope including the size of your budget and staff. Use bullets to express your accomplishments and describe how you perform your job smarter, faster, and more efficiently. Showcase examples of how you help the companies you support make money, save money, save time, improve processes, acquire new business, or keep existing business.

Before: Implemented new CRM system.

After: Implemented new CRM system that improved lead generation by 20% and cut data redundancies in half.

Before: Responsible for revamping new hire payroll processes.

After: Shaved weeks off time required to add new hires to the payroll system and eliminated longstanding payroll redundancies and recurring errors by revamping new hire payroll processes and streamlining data collection.

2. The statistics dump. These resumes show metric after metric –.a 50% increase in sales, a $2M decrease in operating costs, yet they never explain how these stellar results were achieved. The hiring manager needs to understand the story behind your accomplishments, what obstacles you faced and what these statistics mean within a given context in order to be wowed by you.

Tip: Create accomplishments that prove a quantifiable impact and an explanation of the achievement.

Before: Conceived and implemented the Finance First program, achieving $700M in incremental assets.

After: Conceived and implemented the Finance First program, the company's first-ever and most successful integrated marketing program for financial advisory services. Inaugural campaign achieved incremental $700M in assets and earned reputation as the gold standard for all company marketing campaigns.

Before: Attained a 50% increase in funding budget for clinical trials.

After: Attained a 50% increase in funding budget and a renegotiated contract for clinical studies by benchmarking research costs, linking research costs to the unique attributes of the study group, and guaranteeing sponsors an expedited review process and on-time trial start date.

3. The touchy-feely. Most resumes I see start out with an overview paragraph describing the person's personal attributes. Everyone seems to be a dedicated, loyal, hard-worker, not to mention a great communicator and a team player. Yet there is no actual proof that the candidate possesses any of these personal attributes on the resume. Without the proof, these are just words — and a waste of space.

Tip: Create a profile section that focuses on your proven success and the big picture value you can offer an employer. Your profile is like a movie trailer. If the trailer is good, people will want to see the movie. If your profile is compelling, people will want to read the rest of your resume.

Before: Results-producing Marketing professional with a proven record in developing, executing and analyzing comprehensive marketing strategies in support of company goals and objectives. Directed the creation of marketing tools and steered the execution of marketing programs. Demonstrated successful growth in targeted markets through implementation of key projects. Excellent leadership skills; built and guided top-performing marketing teams. Adept at communicating with all levels of management, vendors, and internal departments or partners to coordinate overall marketing efforts. Proven to be reliable, dependable and professional.

After:

Marketing & Operations Professional

consumer goods ▪ retail environments ▪ multi-site locations ▪ corporate & in-store experience ▪ Fortune 500

Marketing Program Management ... Experience launching new products and services and reversing struggling campaigns into strong performing programs with annualized ROI.

Operational Transformations ... Continuous success tightening operational infrastructures to streamline processes, eliminate redundancies, scale resources, optimize staff, and enhance measurement and reporting capabilities.

Leadership ... Reputation for creating programs that motivate staff to collaborate and embrace company mission and values. Demonstrated success in retaining employees, spotting talent, and mentoring high potentials.

The cookie cutter. These are the resumes that were crafted using a template and look like thousands of other resumes. They make you look lazy and just not that into the whole job search gig. They scream, "I don't have an original thought in my head and I like it that way." You don't need to be Picasso to create a resume with a few interesting design elements. The goal is not to use design elements to make the resume look pretty; it is to use design features to make important information stand out.

Tip: Think outside of the box. Create your own resume style to best showcase your information. Don't be afraid to use tables, charts, or graphs if they help get your point across. Step away from the Times New Roman font. There are other good choices for resumes including Arial, Arial Narrow, Calibri, Verdana, and Tahoma.

Before: Improved revenue growth, client growth, loan commitments, and deposit growth significantly during tenure.

After:

Year	Revenue Growth	Client Growth	Loan Commitments	Deposit Growth
2004	5%	5%	$100M	5%
2005	10%	7%	$200M	10%
2006	25%	12%	$300M	15%
2007	30%	22%	$400M	20%
2008	35%	28%	$500M	25%
2009	40%	35%	$600M	30%

Does Your Resume Font Matter?

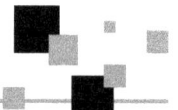

I've heard from frustrated job seekers saying the font shouldn't matter. And maybe it shouldn't. But it does.

Recruiters and hiring managers are sifting through dozens, maybe even hundreds of resumes every day. If the font is too small, too bold, or too fancy they may just skip your resume in favor of something easier to read. If your font is too whimsical or childish, or all caps, they may just question your judgment.

Put yourself in the reader's shoes. Have you ever gone to multiple websites searching for a product or service? Do the aesthetics of the site influence the amount of time you stay on the site? If key information is difficult to find, do you spend a lot of time looking for it or do you move on to the next site? If the site has annoying pop ups or distracting music, do you click away quickly? If the site doesn't look very professional, do you question the quality of the service they are offering? Yes, you do.

It's no different with resumes. The way they look is an important part of your professional brand. Select a font and resume style that is easy to read so the decision maker stays engaged and hopefully contacts you for an interview.

Writing a Resume That Cuts to the Chase

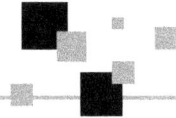

When it comes to resumes, longer is rarely better. In today's fast-paced world, hiring managers generally spend less than 15 seconds looking at a resume. They want to be able to see your key differentiators quickly, and they will rarely look past page two to find the information they need. So how do you keep your resume concise without sacrificing clarity or quality? Here are some common resume problems that can result in a document that is too long and some recommended fixes.

A long job history

If you've been working for 20 years or more, it can seem like a difficult task to craft a resume that is only two pages. This can be accomplished without sacrificing the quality or accuracy of the document. One strategy is to create a separate category for all employment experiences that are more than 15 years old and group them in a section labeled *Early Career Experience* or *Additional Experience*. This section allows you to summarize early experience in just a few sentences and save space for more recent and relevant information.

Additional Experience

Prior executive leadership experience with XYZ Company as Vice President of Sales (1990 to 1996) and five year career with ABC Corporation progressing in various sales, sales management, and corporate marketing positions.

Multiple temporary or consulting assignments

If you have worked multiple assignments during a short period of time, your resume can become confusing for your reader, and the short gigs can make you look like a job-hopper at first glance. To remedy this, create a category called Temporary Assignments or Consulting Assignments and give an overview of the highlights of the experience rather than listing the details of each.

HR Consultant, various assignments 2008 to Present

XYZ Company. For global technology solutions company, selected to create U.S. recruitment strategy for division representing 1,500 employees in six offices. Trimmed recruiting budget (projected savings of 25-50%) using *non-fee, referral, and social media recruitment strategies. Recruited team to support $17M in new business.*

ABC Company. Developed the business strategy and execution plan for an alternative candidate sourcing model that minimized agency costs and leveraged online networking and employee referral programs to deliver $100K in savings in first 5 months of implementation.

Too much information about job tasks

Resumes can become unruly if you include long lists of job responsibilities followed by long lists of accomplishments. To prune your document, create a paragraph of no more than 5 or 6 sentences to explain your job tasks and only bullet your key accomplishments. This strategy will save space and allow your reader to focus on your most important achievements.

Create the strategic direction and execution plans to support large scale corporate events and product launches. Oversee all pre and on-site communications and advertising, media planning, exhibit construction, invitation management, VIP hospitality, sponsor management, and exhibit construction. Manage relationships with 5 advertising agencies. Budget: $10M; Staff: 3 direct reports, 10 indirect reports

- Recognized with Marketing Award in 2011 for orchestrating the company's most successful campaign at the country's premier sports event while trimming event costs by 10%.

- Project-managed product marketing campaign at an international ski resort resulting in 30,000 qualified leads in just 3 months and a 5% conversion rate.

Dedicating equal space to every job experience

Just because you've held seven jobs over the course of your career doesn't mean you should dedicate the same amount of space to each job. Focus on relevance and generally spend more time explaining more recent positions than those held earlier in your career.

Poor use of white space and fonts

Sometimes resumes become too long because of poor decisions about design. Don't create margins that exceed one inch on any side, and use a font of either 10 or 11 points.

10 Reasons to Use a Resume Template (Not!)

Over the past few years, it seems like companies that offer resume templates for job seekers keep popping up and I can understand why. Writing a resume is not an easy undertaking and there is certainly a market for inexpensive tools that appear to make the process a little bit easier. Therefore, if your goals mirror the ones below, maybe a resume template is for you.

1. You want your resume to scream, "Pick me! I'm just like everyone else."

2. You want to prove to a prospective employer that you are not creative.

3. You want everyone who reads your resume to realize that your intention was to spend as little time as possible on the project.

4. You want to show just how well you can cut corners.

5. You want people to know that writing was never your strong suit.

6. You want to showcase as many resume cliché phrases as possible.

7. You dig tacky clip art and dated formats.

8. You are "wowed" by the cheap price tag.

9. You are convinced that no one is interested in seeing your authentic self.

10. You want to remain in the job search as long as possible.

Writing a compelling resume requires you to be introspective about your past accomplishments. It requires that you communicate your stories of success and put those stories in a forward-thinking context that proves to employers that your past experiences can be leveraged to deliver exceptional results for a new company. Many people need help translating their accomplishments into "resumeize" but a template is not the solution. Find a living, breathing professional resume writer to help you rather than a digital tool. By collaborating with a writer, you can create a document that represents the real you and is customized for your particular job search goals.

7 Things You Don't Want to Have on Your Resume

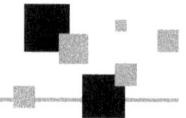

While every job seeker is unique, here are some general items I recommend leaving off your resume to achieve optimal results.

1. **Objectives**

Most hiring managers I talk to are not interested in reading resume objectives. Frequently objectives sound very clichéd and they rarely communicate what a candidate can do for an employer.

Instead, use a professional summary that outlines your competencies and proves how you can help solve business problems.

2. **Months of employment**

Generally, employers are only interested in knowing the year you started and ended employment with a company. Reporting the exact month along with the year is unnecessary. The exception to this rule is if you have been with a company for less than two years. In that case, include the month and year so they can accurately gauge how many months you were employed in a short-tenured position.

3. **References**

The term "references available upon request" is dated and unnecessary on the resume. Employers know that you will supply references if asked.

4. **Hobbies**

Unless you have a hobby that is in some way related to your job target, it's usually best not to mention these. The fact that you enjoy reading and traveling is rarely of interest to the hiring manager.

5. **Your picture**

In a U.S. job market, pictures should not be included on a resume. Hiring managers legally cannot consider your picture in determining if you are to be interviewed or hired, and many companies won't even consider resumes that are submitted with a picture to ensure they are in compliance with Equal Opportunity Employer legislation.

6. **Salary**

Including salary information on your resume generally works against you. When included, a hiring manager may use this information to benchmark whether or not the candidate falls within the salary range of their open position. Since a past salary is only an indication of your earnings in a particular job at a particular point in time, it really isn't an accurate reflection of what you should be paid in another job.

If you apply to an open job and they request a salary history, list a salary range in your cover letter instead to give you a bit more wiggle room if you are called in for an interview.

7. **Your GPA**

Generally, as you gain work experience, your GPA becomes irrelevant to hiring managers. No one will care if you had a 3.8 GPA in 1992 if you can't prove recent success in the positions you have held since then.

Unless you are a recent college graduate, keep your GPA off your resume. And if you are a recent college graduate, only include your GPA if it is a 3.0 or better.

How to Communicate Difficult Stories on Your Resume

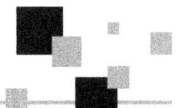

I encourage my clients to tell me authentic stories about their work experiences so I can craft a strong resume for them. Frequently, they shy away from telling stories about disastrous departments, sluggish sales, failed projects, or difficult relationships because they think their story has to be sanitized in order to be acceptable to a hiring manager. But I disagree. Job seekers can show their ability to influence positive outcomes, even when the deck is stacked against them and business conditions are exceptionally challenging. Here are some examples of such situations and how information can be presented in a positive way under challenging circumstances.

Selling in a challenging market...

Secured sales meetings with 80% of target audience; successfully introduced products and services despite inherent obstacles including saturated and shrinking market.

Providing leadership in environments plagued with infighting...

Successfully broke down business silos and improved information sharing across cross-functional teams by creating an open and transparent work environment to foster collaboration.

Salvaging a damaged client relationship...

Reversed strained client relationship that was damaged due to a previous producer's missed deadline by quickly mobilizing team resources to shave close to 75% off the normal project completion time.

Preparing for a failed company's closing...

Developed a liquidation strategy that maximized profit margin from inventory and kept vendors and staff engaged until final closing.

Managing poor performers...

Reversed performance issues for a struggling employee who went on to become the division's #1 account executive and ranked in the top-ten firm-wide.

What are your harrowing work stories and what positive outcomes can be drawn from them?

Resume Writing Tips for Susan Lucci and Others Who Haven't Looked for a Job in Forty Years

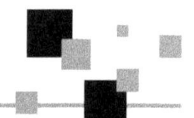

The soap opera *All My Children* was cancelled in 2011 and Susan Lucci played the role of Erica Kane since the show's inception 41 years ago. Four decades with one employer. Certainly not the norm anymore, but there are still many people with exceptionally long tenure in one company. How do you report a 40-year career and avoid age bias? You certainly can't just cut off the first 20 years as if it never happened. Dates of employment are generally confirmed during a routine reference check and claiming your career began in 1990 when in fact it began in 1970 isn't going to fly. Here are 12 tips for crafting a resume if you haven't written one in decades.

1. **Always include your e-mail address.** If there is no e-mail address listed on your resume, it will be more difficult for an employer to contact you quickly, so they may just pass you up in favor of the next candidate who

listed an e-mail address. Even though mainstream e-mail is less than 20 years old, you will look ancient if you don't include an e-mail address.

2. **Include links to social media profiles.** Social media has gained enormous traction over the past few years, and many believe that its use will eventually surpass or even replace e-mail. Be current by creating a LinkedIn profile and displaying the URL within your contact information. Or go one step further and include your Twitter handle, or Skype and instant message names.

3. **Don't make your years of experience the focal point of your top summary.** Eliminate phrases such as "over 25 years of experience" or "seasoned professional." If you have had a 25-year career but the last 10 years have been in a specific industry or function, focus on that rather than the total number of years.

4. **Dedicate more space to explaining your recent experience.** If you have held six jobs over the past 25 years, don't dedicate the same amount of space on the resume to each job. Weight the resume toward your most recent experience (the past 10 years). For a one-page resume, your more recent experience should take up at least half of the page. For a two-page resume (often necessary for someone with more than a 10-year work history), the more recent experience should generally take up the entire first page.

5. **Consolidate early experience.** Account for early work experience to keep the chronology consistent and transparent, but abbreviate this experience when possible. You can include a section called "early career" or "additional experience" and provide an overview of your earlier jobs. For example, a district sales manager might include a statement that says something like, "held sales assistant and regional sales positions at between 1985 and 1992."

6. **Don't hide graduation dates.** If you are thinking about eliminating the year you graduated from high school or college from the resume in an attempt to hide your age, my advice is proceed with caution. When you eliminate the date, you are actually calling more attention to the very thing you are trying to hide. Without the graduation date, an employer may wonder why the date is missing or think you are older than you really are since they have no point of reference for knowing what occurred between the last position listed on the resume and your graduation date. And even if you make it past the initial resume screening and are called in for an interview, once the interviewer realizes that you are older than your resume suggests, you have potentially damaged the trust — which could impede the interview process moving forward. Include a subtle and brief education section; be transparent and move on.

7. **Include hobbies that support an active lifestyle.** Generally, I recommend only including hobbies on a resume if they are relevant. But for the older worker, hobbies that suggest a vibrant and healthy lifestyle may help counter any potential age bias. Therefore, if you are an avid runner, skier, triathlete, etc. go ahead and include this information on your resume.

8. **List current technical skills if relevant.** If you are proficient in Excel or some other program that is important to your job, say so. Don't list outdated programs like Word Perfect or list the Internet as a technology that you are proficient in. At this point, this is the equivalent of writing that you know how to use a telephone.

9. **Eliminate ancient phrases.** Avoid phrases on the resume such as "references available upon request." This is a dated concept and employers know that if they want you to provide references they can ask you for them. Some won't even ask you; they will just Google you and see what they can find out about you online. Other dated phrases include "responsible for," "duties included," "managed day-to-day operations," and "out-of-the-box thinker." These phrases are old and tired — the opposite of the impression you are trying to convey.

10. **Use an updated resume format.** When I see Courier 10 on a resume I am quickly transported back to the days of the manual return and white out. Choose a more updated font such as Arial, Arial Narrow, Times New Roman, Calibri, or Tahoma. Courier 10 and white out should stay in the past where they belong.

11. **Eliminate the resume objective.** No one wants to see an objective on a resume anymore. They communicate what you are looking for, which isn't of much interest to a hiring manager. Hiring authorities want to know what's in it for them…do you have the competencies and the proof of performance to help solve their business problems. Create a profile or executive summary outlining your big picture accomplishments and the value you can bring to an employer instead and leave the objective off the resume.

12. **Don't left justify employment dates.** Having dates of employment to the left made sense in the days of the typewriter when tabs were the only way to indent content. Thanks to Microsoft Word, text is much more malleable and space can be better utilized. Place employment dates after the company name or to the right to optimize space and save room for other important content.

Barbara Safani

Phrases That Kill Resumes

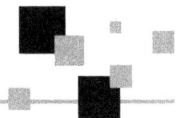

Over my career, I have come into contact with thousands of people who perform miracles at work every day. But you would never know it if you looked at their resumes. More than 90% of the resumes I see overuse personal attributes to describe the person's candidacy.

While personal attributes are factored into the hiring decision, what needs to be communicated on the resume is your value proposition and proof of past successes that demonstrate that these attributes are core to your brand and personal pitch. The words themselves are meaningless unless they are backed up with facts. Here are a few word choices that I frequently see on resumes that unfortunately tell me nothing about you.

Dynamic: If you were so dynamic, you wouldn't be using the word dynamic to describe yourself. Instead, you would be showcasing an accomplishment that proves this quality. For example, maybe you have been able to woo difficult to land clients or you deliver engaging presentations to standing room only crowds.

Trustworthy: What does this mean exactly? That you won't share proprietary information or you won't steal post-its from the company's supply closet? If you chose to put that word on your resume, there must have been a reason you selected it. Think about the success stories that prove why being trustworthy is important for the work you do and write about that instead.

Team Player: This one really makes me cringe. It's so stale it leads me to believe that you haven't thought about your resume since 1987. Tell me how you collaborate with others, mentor staff, recommend initiatives that make teams more cohesive... anything, but please don't just tell me you are a team player.

Strong Communication Skills: Right. You are such a great communicator that the words alone make it true. Where's the communications piece in this equation? Please communicate to me what you have done that proves this skill. That's what a strong communicator does.

Stop selling yourself short by relying on these phrases that kill resumes. Instead, focus on the accomplishment-based examples of your work that make you a star.

Is Your Resume a Turkey?

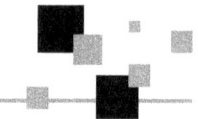

Many people with great job skills and noteworthy achievements have resumes that are poorly written and fail to market their candidacy appropriately. Is your resume a turkey? Compare your document content against these common resume mistakes.

Task Overload

Most people's resumes have exhaustive lists of job tasks but never chronicle how those job tasks contributed to the bottom line for the company. Without an accomplishment focused resume, your document is bound to get lost in a sea of mediocrity. Stand out from the crowd by showcasing examples of how you help the companies you support make money, save money, and save time.

An exercise to help you think of your experiences in terms of accomplishments is to identify the problems or challenges you faced on the job, the actions you took to overcome the obstacles, and the results achieved by your actions. By creating these stories, you capitalize on what makes you unique, rather than dwelling on the tasks that are part of many people's jobs and only make you forgettable.

Claustrophobic Text

Good content helps make a good resume. However, sometimes people include so much content in the resume that they sacrifice design and end up with a document that has so much text that it suffocates the reader. Choose a font size no smaller than 10 point and break the text up by using bullets and spaces rather than big blocky paragraphs. Keep the margins to at least .6 on all sides. These strategies will make your document more "user friendly" and encourage the hiring manager to read on.

Spell-check Suicide

Many recruiters and hiring managers agree that having a typo on a resume is the fastest way to get placed in the "no" pile. It can be hard to review your own resume. By the time you finish it, you are so close to the situation that it can be hard to spot errors. Here are a few suggestions for catching those pesky typos.

1. **Use spell-check wisely.** Spell-check is a great tool, but supplement spell-check with several human rounds of proofreading.

2. **Read the document backwards.** Doing so forces you to slow down and pay attention to each word rather than skimming the sentence.

3. **Ask a friend or trusted colleague to proofread the document.** It's amazing what a fresh set of eyes will spot.

4. **Get an 8th grade English teacher to read your resume.** Okay, maybe they are harder to come by, but they will know it all when it comes to spelling and grammar.

Email Etiquette

Your email address is part of your professional image and a critical piece of information on your resume. Email addresses that are cute, silly, provocative, or difficult to key just won't cut it with hiring managers. Chose an address that is some combination of your first and last name and avoid using long strings of numbers or letters that don't form a word. Email addresses are part of your professional persona. You want to stand out from the crowd because of your unique accomplishments, not your unusual email address. Keep it simple and professional and you will quickly elevate your credibility with hiring authorities.

Resume Renovations

While many resumes adequately explain a job seeker's job responsibilities, few elaborate on the accomplishments within those responsibilities. Let's face it, many people perform similar jobs with similar competencies. What makes each person unique is the success he or she brought to those positions, not the day-to-day tasks that hundreds of others may be trained to do. Consider these typical resume statements from job seekers who probably have a great deal to offer employers, but are not getting that message across in their documents.

'Answered questions that pertained to each customer's needs.'

Undoubtedly, customer service is critical for many positions. But this statement tells the reader little, other than that a function of the job was answering questions. Hiring managers want to know the volume of inquiries, how long did it take to resolve customer issues and how did that timeframe compare to the company's standards. Are there any powerful examples of how an irate client was satisfied, and were any processes put in place to address redundant questions to free up time to work on more complex issues?

'Develop and execute promotional opportunities.'

Great! Tell me more! What types of campaigns and what were the results? Did the promotions drive revenues, capture a new niche, or take market share away from a competitor? What was going on in the company before these promotions were developed and what is happening now as a result of them?

'Prepared weekly reporting on equipment performance.'

Why were the reports prepared and who received them? Was the report used by senior management for forecasting or decisions on vendor contracts? Was any money or time saved as a result of these reports and if so, how much?

'Develop business plans and strategies to build rapport and solicit new business accounts.'

Sounds important. What were the results? Was new business secured, and if so, what was the percent increase in accounts from last year until now and what were the revenues associated with that new business? Were creative strategies or guerrilla marketing techniques leveraged to obtain the business?

Break away from the day to day of your work experience and strive to showcase the unique, memorable, creative, and "above and beyond" moments. You will quickly rise to the top of the resume pile and secure more interviews faster.

Create an Authentic and Ethical Resume to Win the Job

A resume is a marketing tool and I encourage job seekers to position their accomplishments in the best possible light. However, it is critical that all information reported on the document is accurate and something you can back up with facts if questioned. Here are some of the ways I see job candidates crossing the line of ethical resume writing practices and some suggestions for creating a more authentic presentation of your qualifications.

Exaggerated results.

Never make up business results assuming no one will be able to validate them. You must be able to back up any information you write on your resume with proof during the interview. However, this does not mean that you must have exact figures in order to mention the accomplishment on the resume. It is fine to show results with approximate dollars, percentages, or numbers as long as you can have a discussion around how these results were achieved. The goal is to show impact, not statistics. For example, if you know you used to spend at least 4 hours per week on a particular task and you then automated the process and it is now done in the click of a button, it is fine to say that you decreased time spent on this task by 4 hours or that you virtually eliminated the time spent on this task.

Claiming full ownership of a project.

Frequently our accomplishments are achieved as part of a team effort. Never claim full ownership of a large-scale initiative if the results should be attributed to the team. Use phrases such as "as part of a team", "co-producer", "co-author", etc. to clearly communicate your value without misrepresenting your achievements.

Making up job titles.

If you were in a director role, don't state that you were the SVP. However if your job title was not truly representative of your responsibilities, consider tweaking the title to make it more relevant or putting an alternative title in parenthesis.

Fudging dates.

Don't alter dates to make a gap look shorter. Most hiring authorities are interested in the number of years you were employed at an organization, not the months and years, so consider just using years to record your chronology, but be prepared to discuss the exact dates if asked. If the gap spans a year or more, create a clear explanation of what you were doing during that time period right on the resume. For example if you were caring for your children or a sick parent, be transparent and say that on the resume.

Listing a degree you never earned.

Information on degrees is pretty easy to verify. If you attended college but didn't graduate, list the course of study, school name, and location, but leave the degree off.

Putting jargon on your resume you can't support.

If you have added keywords to your resume to describe your competencies, make sure you know the meaning of those keywords and can explain them during an interview. Don't just copy them from a job posting or someone else's resume because they "sounded good." You will compromise your credibility with the hiring authority if you can't speak to everything on your resume.

Does Your Resume Make You Look Like A Job Hopper?

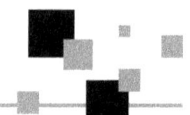

When hiring managers read resumes, one of the first things they look at is dates of employment. If they see multiple short employment stints, they will often assume that you are a job hopper, question your ability to stay at one company for long, and move on to the next candidate.

Often people's choppy employment record may be caused by several factors beyond their control, but unless the story behind your job changes is made clear on the resume, you risk being passed over for someone who can offer the perception of a more stable work chronology. Here are some of the circumstances that make job seekers look like job hoppers and what you can do about it.

Serial layoffs. It happens. You may be a loyal employee, but perhaps you have been the victim of serial layoffs and as a result, your resume depicts movement every year or two. Rather than just putting your dates of employment on the resume and letting hiring managers come to their own conclusions as to why you left, tell them why right on the resume. Add a brief explanation following the dates of employment — such as "company downsized," "company relocated," or "company went out of business." This way, the employer has the facts and isn't left to guess why you are no longer with the company.

Temporary assignments. If you have spent the past few years working on consulting or temporary assignments, your chronology may be questionable to your reader. Instead of listing each temporary assignment and company with their corresponding employment dates, create one category for temporary assignments with the total length of time you have been working in this capacity. Then give an overview of the companies you have supported and highlight some of the main accomplishments that encompass all of your temporary experience.

Rapid promotions. Frequently I see resumes where the person has been at the same company for 10-plus years, and they re-list the company name and new job title and dates each time they are promoted. To the reader who is quickly scanning the document, this may cause confusion; he may think these were positions at different companies. Just because it is obvious to you, don't assume it is obvious to the reader who may be trying to get through hundreds of resumes. List the company name once and place the full dates of employment to the far right. Underneath that, list each job title with the employment dates immediately following. By placing full dates of employment and dates of specific company positions in different sections, you increase the chances that the reader will understand that these changes were the result of promotions at the same company and not job changes.

Company mergers. Have you worked for a company that was bought by another company and then bought by another in less than five years? When you list all three company names individually with the dates you worked for each company, it can look like you voluntarily went to work for each of these companies during that short time frame. A better strategy is to list the current name of the company and in parenthesis write "formerly company XYZ" and follow that with the full dates of employment from the time you started at the first company before any acquisitions occurred.

The bottom line is this: Employers don't read resumes. They scan them very quickly, and it's easy to have your information misinterpreted if you do not make things crystal clear for your reader. Obviously, there is more of a story to tell behind your employment experience and the reasons why you changed jobs. But in order to be able to tell that story to a hiring manager, you need to make sure that your resume provides enough of a positive hook that they decide to call you in for an interview.

One Typo You Should Have on Your Resume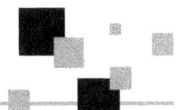

I've frequently received mail from readers infuriated by the fact that many job seekers and career professionals write the word resume rather than resume with the accent marks over the two "és." The grammar police can be seen out in full force on some occasions, and some people seem to revel in making their case by hyperlinking to the word's definition and proper spelling as shown in Merriam-Webster Online.

But there is actually a reason *not* to use the accent marks on the word resume in the online world. Many employers ask that resumes be copied and pasted into text boxes on their website, so they can be uploaded and tracked via the company's applicant tracking system. But when you convert the word resume with the accent marks into plain text, it shows up as r?sum?.

.. Ouch, now that *does* look like a typo!

That's not the only symbol that may not convert properly in a text-only format. You know those lovely bullets you have in front of each key point on your resume? They often change into question marks as well, once the document is converted into text. Imagine showcasing a great achievement like, "reduced costs by $1M dollars, in one year" and having that point show up with a question mark, almost as if you are questioning whether you really accomplished this feat at all!

If you plan on uploading your resume on sites that don't give you the option of including a Word attachment, or if you need to copy your resume and cover letter into a text box or e-mail, here's what you need to know about creating a text only version of your resume that reads properly.

1. Save your Word document in .txt format (ASCII).

2. Save document as text with line breaks.

3. Set the page formatting to 60 characters per line.

4. Omit bold, italics, and underlining from the document.

5. Change double quotes to single quotes.

6. Remove tabs, columns, and bullets and save document with single line space breaks.

7. Eliminate non-ASCII symbols such as bullet points.

8. Convert document to a fixed width font such as Courier New 12 point.

9. Use spaces to line up texts instead of tabs.

10. Left justify text; center text through use of spacing

That's certainly much better than sending an introductory letter that says, "My r?sum? is attached for your review." By the way, if you are wondering why I omitted using the accent marks in the word resume while writing this, it's because the search engines don't read the accent marks properly either. And since most people search for this type of content using the search term resume and not r?sum? I thought this too was a good reason to have a "typo" in this section.

5 Resume Formatting Mistakes to Avoid

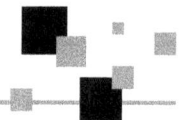

Hiring managers may have to sift through hundreds of resumes before they find the person they want to call in for the interview. So many resumes I see would be passed over quickly by a hiring manager simply because they are too difficult to read. Here are five resume formatting mistakes to avoid.

1. **Too chunky.** Big blocks of text on a resume are hard to read. Short digestible sound bites work better. Use a brief paragraph (no more than six lines) to describe your job responsibilities, but place your main accomplishments and rich examples of how you have helped the companies you supported make money, save money, or save time in an easy-to-read bulleted list.

2. **Too tiny.** If you are using a font smaller than 10 point on your resume, it is too small. No one will take the time to get out his or her magnifying glass. If space is an issue, try readjusting the margins or using a tighter font.

3. **Too fancy.** Certain fonts are more difficult to read than others. Stay away from fonts that resemble script or are overly ornate. Avoid uncommon fonts that may display differently on the receiver's end. Arial and Times New Roman are generally safe choices.

4. **Too tight.** White space is important on a resume. Be sure to leave ample space in between company names and the different sections of the resume to make it easy for your reader to spot key breaks in the document.

5. **Too long.** If you have important information about your professional background that doesn't appear on the resume until page 3 or later, it's time to prune the document. Few people will read a third page. If you have an extended chronology, abbreviate earlier positions or create a category called "additional experience" that provides an overview of earlier positions in a brief paragraph.

5 Resume Tricks That Will Make You Stand Out

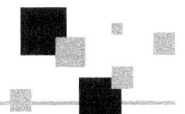

Tired of having a resume that doesn't seem to "wow" hiring managers? Get ready to be bold and take some risks with the presentation of your professional qualifications to spice up your resume, entice hiring managers and get the phone to ring. Here are five ways to turn that big yawn of a resume into a powerful and vibrant self-marketing tool.

1. Add accomplishments.

The cornerstone of a strong resume is the content. Hiring managers don't want to read long lists of job tasks. They need to know how you have helped the companies you supported do things smarter, faster and more efficiently.

Don't simply write about your job responsibilities; write about impact. Try to show the before-and-after picture of your work and whenever possible, use dollars, numbers and percentages to show how you made money, saved money, or saved time.

2. Key in on keywords.

Keywords are the buzzwords for your industry or profession. Hiring managers and the applicant tracking systems that frequently scan resumes search for these keywords. Without them, you may never land the interview.

Review job postings of positions that match your skill set and mirror the keywords in the job descriptions in your resume. You can achieve this by adding an "areas of expertise" section or weaving the keywords throughout the content of your resume.

3. Test out a testimonial.

Including testimonials about your work from supervisors, clients and vendors that prove the value you brought to an organization can go a long way on a resume. Few job seekers include these endorsements on their resume, assuming no one is interested.

Hiring managers frequently review endorsements on candidate's LinkedIn profiles, and some even sort candidates based on the number of endorsements they have. If endorsements are searched on a LinkedIn profile, chances are good they will be read on your resume.

4. Don't be afraid of design.

Design elements such as bold, shading, boxes, graphs, charts and images can be used on a resume to make a more powerful presentation, convey quality information in a small amount of space, or just differentiate your candidacy from the 500 other resumes sitting on the hiring manager's desk. An engaging resume doesn't look like everyone else's. It stands out from the crowd.

5. Link to social media profiles.

You can make your resume more three-dimensional by including links to your social media profiles within the contact information section of the resume. By adding your LinkedIn URL, you can direct your reader to additional information about you, showcase more detailed testimonials than you may be able to fit on your resume, share information on the groups you belong to and even display samples of your work.

If you are active on Twitter, you can include your handle on your resume, which is a great way to show employers your passion for what you do, your thought leadership, and the way you engage within a community. Social media can turn a static one-dimensional resume into a multidimensional, real-time representation of who you are and what you have to offer the employer.

Questions to Ask Yourself Before Writing Your Resume

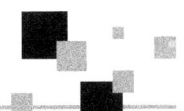

It can be hard to reflect on your accomplishments and articulate them clearly on just one or two pieces of paper. But being introspective about your past and thinking about what you have achieved is critical to putting together a strong resume. Here are some questions to ask yourself to generate more powerful content for your resume:

1. Do you manage a staff? How large is it? Do you manage a budget? What is the size of the budget?

2. What specific professional challenges did you face when you took this job. Do you have specific performance goals? How well did you do against these goals?

3. What was the most difficult project you managed or biggest hurdle you overcame at this job? What were the results and benefits for you and the organization?

4. Have you decreased costs or streamlined operations in some way? How was this accomplished? Wherever possible, state your accomplishments in terms of a numerical value, ideally in terms of either a dollar value or percentage.

5. What is your greatest achievement in this position? How did you do it? What were results and benefits to you and the organization?

6. Did you receive any special awards or recognitions? If so, for what?

7. What have your supervisors said about your performance, either in evaluations or verbally?

Another exercise for thinking about your accomplishments is to create CAR stories.

C -- Challenge: What challenges did you face in your job?
A -- Action: What actions did you take to address those challenges?
R -- Results: What results were achieved because of your actions?

Here are a few examples of strong accomplishment statements that were created by asking achievement-focused questions and creating CAR stories.

For a claims administrator ...

- Recouped $33K in benefits payments and worker's compensation claims by auditing benefits status and meticulously managing paperwork to verify employee eligibility. (demonstrates how the applicant saved money)

For a customer service manager ...

- In just six months, propelled customer satisfaction scores by 16 points from 78% to 94% (highest scores in account history) and reversed failing account performing from 15% below target to exceeding target. (shows how the applicant retained business and clients)

For a sales professional ...

- Increased renewal rate by 23%, with a 4% year-over-year order growth rate, despite a downturn in the pharmaceutical industry. Attained record sales results in 2010. (shows how the candidate improved retention)

For an HR manager ...

- Saved company tens of thousands of dollars in recruiting fees and close to a quarter of a million dollars in benefits costs by renegotiating terms of service with outsourced providers. (shows how money was saved)

For a service administrator ...

- In less than two months reduced warranty expenses from 25% to 1% by streamlining reporting process and using an online warranty application to expedite the claims process. (shows how a process was improved)

Take the time to ask yourself questions that focus on your accomplishments over job tasks. You will improve the quality of your resume and your overall job search.

How to Address Employment Gaps on a Resume

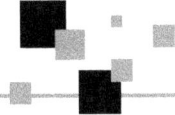

Many people ask me how to address a significant gap in employment due to caring for a sick family member, coping with an extended illness or raising a family.

In this situation, it is best to be transparent and explain what you have been doing during this period of time. It is better to account for the time away from the work world on your resume than to neglect to reference the employment gap and let employers come to their own (and possibly incorrect) conclusions.

In addition, there are several strategies you can use to shift the focus away from the employment gap and toward your unique message of value. Here are a few suggestions:

1. Showcase unpaid experience.

Just because you didn't hold a paid position during the time you were not working doesn't mean you haven't done any work that has provided value to someone. Perhaps you helped a spouse or family member with business tasks or ran events at your children's school. Maybe you did work at local community center or place of worship.

2. Focus on transferable skills.

Think about the skills you developed through these volunteer tasks. Perhaps you built up skills as a homemaker or volunteer in project management, event planning, administration, fund-raising, web design, travel arrangements, teaching or cooking. These valuable skills are easily transferable to paid opportunities.

3. Don't forget to tout your past career experience.

Just because you haven't used a skill in a few years doesn't mean that the skill is obsolete. Describe what you did in your past jobs that is still relevant in the current market. For example, if you used quantitative customer service skills in your last position, these skills will still be relevant.

4. Find others who can sing your praises.

Gather testimonials from organizations where you have done volunteer work or from friends and family you may have helped with a project and include this information on your resume. These testimonials can showcase a candidate's personal and professional attributes in an authentic way and elevate your skill set in the eyes of the employer.

5. Embrace social media.

Make it easier for hiring managers and recruiters to find you by creating searchable online profiles on the top social media and online identity sites. You don't have to be currently working to have a profile on LinkedIn, ZoomInfo, or Google profiles.

Functional Resumes Should be Re-Named Dysfunctional Resumes

Recently, someone showed me a resume and asked for a critique. The resume had absolutely no chronology, no company names, position titles, or dates of employment. It simply grouped work experience into categories with no reference to where this experience occurred. When I asked her why this information was omitted, she replied by saying, "I don't need to include that information; it's a functional resume."

Many years ago, someone came up with the idea of the functional resume -- a resume that merely focused on functional skills and eliminated all references to employment experience. The logic was that this would better display a candidate's transferable functional skills and eliminate the need to explain away problems in the person's chronology such as employment gaps or experience that wasn't related to the job target.

But at its core, the functional resume is truly dysfunctional. Recruiters and hiring managers are immediately suspect of resumes without a chronology and few will even bother to review them. Most will draw their own conclusions about why certain information was omitted and you will never get a chance to explain your strategy.

So what do you do if you are transitioning careers or have an employment gap that would be glaring on a chronological resume? Go for what's called a combination format. Use functional categories to show your relevant skills and accomplishments but supplement that with an abbreviated chronology that shows company names, job titles, and employment dates. Whenever possible, explain employment gaps right on the resume with brief explanations such as "company downsized" or "left position to care for a sick parent." It is always better to be transparent because it reduces the likelihood that the reader will draw their own conclusions from your omissions.

Also, keep in mind that if you are focusing on your functional skills because you are making a career transition, a resume alone may not be enough to validate that transition. Everyone in a job search needs supporters, but career changers and people with questionable chronologies need them even more. A piece of paper can't always explain away all the questions a hiring authority may have about your qualifications for a job where you have limited experience. Career changers build that type of trust by asking people close to the decision makers to make introductions and advocate for their candidacy. Once that is achieved, the resume can be used to help support their value proposition.

So if you've been leaning toward creating a functional resume to position yourself in front of a potential employer, you are probably headed in the wrong direction. Create a combination format and build a network of "cheerleaders" that can help you gain the right introductions to move toward your new career path.

4 Tips for Career Change Cover Letters

A client recently asked, "How do you write a cover letter for a job you have no experience in? It can be difficult to write a cover letter for a position when you don't have any previous experience in that field."

Employers tend to favor candidates with linear careers and those who have proved themselves in similar industries and job functions in the past. However, it's not impossible to change careers, and a strong cover letter can help you gain the attention of the hiring manager. Whenever possible, try to couple your cover letter with a strong networking strategy. Someone who can advocate for your character and potential can be an enormous help when you are trying to make inroads into an industry or job function where you have no previous experience. Here are four tips for writing career change cover letters.

1. **Showcase education that is relevant to your desired job target.**

You may not have any work experience in your new field, but perhaps you have completed coursework to better prepare you for the new role. Focus the cover letter on what was learned in school and include coursework and any school projects that simulated real work experience.

2. **Demonstrate transferable skills to the new position.**

Perhaps you have technology, problem solving, organization, project management, or finance skills that will prove beneficial in the new role. Whenever possible, prove that you already possess a skill set that is highly adaptable to the new work environment.

3. **Leverage any volunteer experience that is similar to the position you are targeting.**

Volunteering is a great way to gain valuable experience that can be positioned on a resume or cover letter. Just because experience isn't paid doesn't mean it isn't relevant.

4. **Explain why you are a good fit for the new position.**

Articulate your reasons for making a career change and why you are passionate about this new role. Show anything from your background that may help prove that you can handle the transition with ease.

Do You Need a Cover Letter?

When I ask hiring managers and recruiters if they read cover letters, their reactions to cover letters are all over the board. So, here are my conclusions:

1. **Half the people you send your cover letter to will probably read it and the other half will not.** Since you can never be sure who your audience is, it is best to cover your bases and send a cover letter.

2. **A strong cover letter might distinguish you in a sea of mediocrity.** Most people's cover letters fail to convey a message of value to the employer. But a strong cover letter can help you customize your resume and grab the attention of a hiring authority.

3. **A resume is fairly formulaic, a cover letter is not.** Cover letters can be used to communicate interest, passion, and enthusiasm regarding a job opening. They are often used to build the initial rapport between the job seeker and the employer.

4. **Specific action-oriented cover letters work better than generic ones full of fluff.** Showcase strong accomplishments that are relevant to your reader and use metrics whenever possible to validate your competencies. Stay away from tired cover letter phrases such as team player, strong communicator, or detail oriented. Hiring authorities assume you have these competencies. Leverage accomplishment statements to prove your success across these competencies.

Ten Tips for Writing Stand-Out Cover Letters

A cover letter is recommended when sending a resume to a hiring manager or recruiter. The letter allows the job seeker to tailor their resume to the open position and start a dialogue with the hiring authority. Here are ten tips for more powerful cover letters.

1. **Begin your cover letter with a compelling statement.** Rather than starting your cover letter with a reference to the position you are applying for, write a statement that aligns your candidacy with the organization, industry, or job function you are targeting.

2. **Minimize the use of the word "I".** Vary your sentences to keep the reader engaged.

3. **Ask for the interview.** Create a strong call to action in your letter by expressing your interest in the company and requesting an in-person interview.

4. **Match your qualifications to the requirements of the job.** Create a cover letter that addresses each job requirement point by point. The stronger the match you can make between the two, the greater the likelihood of securing the interview.

5. **Build rapport with your audience.** Discuss relevant business issues and ask thought provoking questions to show your reader that you recognize their needs.

6. **Include a famous quote to make your point.** Incorporating quotes that are relevant to the topics discussed in your letter is a great way to create an interesting and memorable document.

7. **Keep the letter to one page.** Keep your cover letters short and use short paragraphs and bulleted lists to keep the reader's attention and make it easy for them to determine the match between your qualifications and their open job.

8. **Address the hiring authority by name.** The likelihood of building rapport with the reader and validating your interest in the job is increased when the inside cover address refers to the specific person rather than "Dear Sir". Whenever possible, sleuth around for additional information on the hiring manager so you can personalize your letter.

9. **Reference the position you are applying for.** Be sure to mention the job title and job number in the body of your letter as well as in your email subject line. Many hiring authorities request this information and your inability to follow their instructions could jeopardize your candidacy.

10. **Sign your name.** In this age of email, sometimes people forget to do this. If you are sending a letter regular mail, include your handwritten signature. If your correspondence is via email, create an electronic signature.

Forget the Thank You Letter, Lose the Job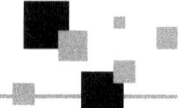

According to a 2011 CareerBuilder survey, 22 percent of the 2,800 employers surveyed said they were less likely to hire a candidate who neglects to send a thank you letter. Of that 22 percent, 86 percent said it showed a lack of follow through and an additional 56 percent said that it sends the message that the candidate isn't really interested in the job. Since you never know how much of a factor the thank you letter may play in the hiring manager's decision, it's always best to send one. Here are some tips for crafting a thank you note that scores points with the hiring manager and keeps you on their radar.

A thank you letter creates an opportunity to reconnect with employers.

Chances are you are one of many candidates being interviewed for an open position. Writing a follow up letter allows you to build a relationship with the interviewer and develop rapport. By expressing your gratitude for the interview and recapping the highlights of the meeting, you revisit the reasons you believe there is an appropriate fit between you and the organization.

Following up keeps your candidacy "top of mind".

Often candidates make the mistake of putting too much control in the interviewer's hands. They believe that if they are the best candidate, the interviewer will remember them and keep them in the loop regarding the selection process. However, this is often not the case. It's critical that candidates remind prospective employers of their interest in a position and the thank you letter is the perfect vehicle for communicating this.

Written correspondence allows you to sell your strengths again.

While part of the reason for the thank you letter is to express gratitude for the meeting, the document serves a much more strategic purpose. It provides an opportunity for the candidate to repackage their skills and accomplishments into another format and market their value added to the employer.

The document enables you to address points you neglected to discuss during the interview.

Many candidates report that after they leave the interview they think of all the other things they could have said during the meeting. Rather than labeling this a liability, turn it into an asset by discussing these points in the thank you letter and remind the reader of your ability to produce similar results for their organization.

A letter helps develop rapport and increases the employer's comfort level with your candidacy.

A good strategy is to recap a part of the conversation where you and the interviewer shared similar views on a job-related topic. The thank you letter can also be a forum for demonstrating your consultative problem solving skills. By addressing current issues the employer is facing and proposing solutions, you are contributing to the company's success even before you are on board.

Thank you letters continue to be an important component of a successful job search campaign. However, the focus has shifted from a simple courtesy and show of appreciation to a targeted self-marketing tool. By creating letters that validate your candidacy, build rapport, and remind the reader of your value added, you can significantly influence potential employers and increase your chances for subsequent interviews.

Is It Acceptable to Send a Thank You Letter Via Email?

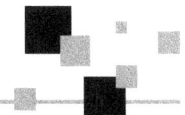

Frequently job seekers ask me if it is appropriate to email a thank you letter after an interview or if snail mail is the preferred method. It is perfectly acceptable to email a thank you letter and sending the letter electronically carries many benefits including:

- **Immediacy.** I recommend sending a thank you letter within 24 hours of a job interview. Email allows you to reconnect with the hiring manager quickly following the interview. Doing so helps you remain top of mind with the hiring manager.

- **Reciprocation.** There is a greater likelihood that a hiring manager will respond to an email than snail mail. By keeping the dialogue open with the hiring manager, you strengthen the relationship and improve your chances of being called in for the next round of interviews.

- **Efficiency.** When you email your thank you letter, the hiring manager can follow your response electronically and easily share it with other members of the team. There is less chance of the document being lost or misplaced as well.

How to Write a Reference List

Job seekers frequently ask me where they should list references on their resume. The answer is that you shouldn't list references anywhere on your resume. References belong on a separate sheet of paper that you can offer to the employer when they ask.

While many employers will ask for your references on the job application, few will call them unless you are a final candidate for the job or are offered a position. At that point, you may need to offer them your reference list. Here is what that list should include.

1. Reference name and job title
2. Company where you worked together
3. Company address (if reference is still employed there)
4. Phone and/or cell number
5. E-mail address
6. Relationship to applicant

It is acceptable to use a reference of someone who is no longer employed by the company where you worked together. The most important factor in a strong reference is that they can vouch for your character and job performance.

Once you know that your references may be contacted, it's important to contact each reference as soon as possible and let them know that they will receive a call from a human resources representative or from a hiring manager. Inform your references of the following:

- The name of the company considering you for hire

- The title of the position for which you are under consideration

- The primary requirements of the position

- Your skills and accomplishments that make you a fit for the position

- Key statements you would like your references to offer in the reference interview

Be sure to send a thank you letter to your reference contacts after they have provided the reference to a potential hiring manager.

I'm Afraid to List My Former Boss as a Reference

Many people tell me they did not have a good working relationship with their former supervisor and they are concerned about using them as a reference on a job application. It's the classic catch 22. If you don't list the supervisor as a reference, the hiring manager may wonder why. If you do list them as a reference, the former supervisor may say something damaging to your candidacy.

What can you do? Here are a few suggestions.

1. **Contact your former human resources representative.** Just because a prospective employer asks for references doesn't mean your former company will actually give one. Many companies have very strict policies about what employees can and cannot say about a former employee. Check with human resources to see what your previous employer's policy is. They may only offer basic reference information such as dates of employment and job title.

2. **Build a portfolio of other, stronger references.** If you absolutely can't use your former boss as a reference, have plenty of other positive references to offer a potential employer. By showing that you have had strong working relationships with other bosses and colleagues in the past, you may mitigate the potential damage caused by one poor reference or at least be able to show that the damaged relationship was an isolated incident.

3. **Hire a reference check service.** If you are worried about what a previous boss might say about you, get a reference checking service such as Allison & Taylor to do a background check for you. This way you can find out what a supervisor would say before you list them as a reference. If the reference is negative, you can have a lawyer send a cease and desist letter to top management at the company. Frequently, once this is done, the problem is solved.

4. **Explain any special circumstances.** Sometimes difficulties with bosses occur due to special circumstances. Perhaps you fell out of favor after accumulating several absences that were unavoidable due to a family or health issue. Or you had recurring car trouble that caused you to be chronically late to work. In situations such as these, it may be in your best interest to explain the circumstances and explain that it was an isolated issue that has since been resolved and won't happen again.

5. **Stay optimistic.** Frequently even if you had a poor relationship with a previous boss, they won't give a damaging reference. Bosses need to be careful of saying anything that could be construed as a defamation of character, and many bosses realize that a poor relationship with a subordinate often reflects badly on them and their managerial capabilities. Often this type of boss says very little during a reference check that would actually be damaging.

What's Holding You Back from Writing a Better Resume?

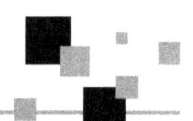

I have met thousands of people who perform miracles at work every day. They pour their heart and soul into their work and offer their employers their knowledge and skills to help make those companies a success. However, you would never know it if you looked at the resumes most people write for themselves. People can usually articulate what they do, but they generally don't convey why what they do as important or who derives value from their actions. They neglect to tie their job tasks to impact. They fail to create a compelling argument for why a hiring manager should give them a chance. The reasons for this vary from person to person, but here are the most common excuses I hear from job seekers. Do any of these sound like you?

1. **I just did my job; I didn't do anything out of the ordinary.** Companies hire people to create positive outcomes for the company. If no positive

outcome is achieved, the person will not last long. Think about what makes you good at what you do and what would happen if you didn't do your job properly. What problems would arise and what opportunities would be lost? Think about the value you bring to the position and the qualities you bring to the job that make you good at what you do.

2. **Writing about what I achieved would be bragging and I don't want people to think I have a swelled head.** A resume is not a list of the things you do or the skills you have. It is a marketing tool and the goal is to entice the reader with enough information to pique their curiosity and get them to ask for more. As long as the information you are presenting is truthful, it's not bragging. Hiring managers may be looking at hundreds of resumes for the same position. They may spend only a few seconds looking at your resume. They are not really reading it, but merely scanning it for relevance, fit, and impact. Your resume needs to communicate these things quickly and with very little effort on the hiring manager's part.

3. **I was in a support role and didn't have any impact on the bottom line.** Think past the tasks associated with the role and reflect on the impact your job had on those around you and the business as a whole. For example, IT professionals build efficiencies within systems to improve the service to the end user. This allows the end user to do their jobs more accurately and faster. Administrative Assistants act as gatekeepers for their bosses and help prioritize their workload so the boss can concentrate on the most mission-critical efforts. The assistant develops systems and processes that help their boss save time.

4. **I'm not sure what impact I had. I never got to see the sales information.** You don't need to have exact figures in order to show impact. It is appropriate to estimate dollars, numbers, and percentages on a resume as long as you can back up those estimates with sound reasoning during the interview. For example, if you streamlined a process that in turn allowed you to create an additional sales cycle or introduce a new product, you should be able to estimate what the increase in new revenue or volume would be. If you automated a process that previously took at least two hours on average to complete and now it is completed with the click of a button, you can certainly show the impact of your actions.

5. **I achieved things as part of a team. I can't take credit for the entire project.** Agreed. You should never embellish your accomplishments or take full credit where it is not due. However, you can say that as part of a team, as co-producer, co-author, etc. that you accomplished something and write about the overall impact of the project you were part of.

6. **I plan to explain the impact of what I do during the interview.** Good luck getting to the interview. Without proof of your accomplishments in the resume, it is unlikely that you will get to plead your case in the interview. Use the resume as the teaser for what's to come in the interview. Give them enough information about your actions and results to leave them wanting more. Don't leave them in the dark and assume they will ask for more if they want it because they probably won't.

7. **I don't want to write too much on my resume about what I did because doing so will make my resume too long.** You can create impact without being verbose. Concentrate on delivering a key metric and a succinct glimpse or the accomplishment and you will be able to keep the resume to a reasonable length.

8. **I just graduated from college and I haven't done any meaningful work yet.** Perhaps you haven't done much paid work yet, but you've certainly done work that will help you prepare for the next steps in your career. Focus on the accomplishments within your coursework, internships, volunteer positions, and leadership roles on campus.

9. **I know I had an impact , but I have no idea how to quantify it.** Take a look at previous years' performance reviews for indicators of your impact or talk to colleagues about projects you worked on. Impact isn't just about the numbers. Perhaps you introduced some "first-ever" initiatives or reversed an "at-risk" relationship with a client. Discuss the successes within these accomplishments and use phrases such as "significantly improved" or "substantially reduced" to prove impact.

10. **I was not in my job long enough to show impact *or* the last company I was with failed and there is little opportunity for me to show stories of success.** You may still be able to discuss projected results or impact for a company where your tenure was short. If the company was struggling, write about what you did contribute. Perhaps you set up the company's first infrastructure or built the company's sales pipeline from the ground up. Separate your successes from the failures of the company, and if possible, back those successes up with a quote from a supervisor, client, or vendor.

Break free of these resume writing excuses and instead opt for creating a resume that focuses on your strong stories of success and measurable achievements.

6 Ways to Fix Resume Formatting Mistakes and Save Space

Creating a resume where all the content lays out on the page in a way that is easy to read and visually appealing can be challenging. Sometimes in their quest to get all the content on one or two pages, the writer resorts to using design strategies such as a smaller font, tighter margins, or compressed spacing to trim the document. But these strategies are flawed and can make the resume harder to read. Others allow the content to spill over to a second or third page with just a few lines of text on that page. This looks unprofessional and on some level may suggest that you ran out of things to say, which is certainly not the message you want to convey. Here are some tips for pruning content to create a tight but easy to read, visually appealing resume.

1. **Streamline contact information.** Many resumes I see lay out the contact information on 5 or more lines. There is no rule that says the information must be communicated in this way. You can list your name on one line and your address, phone numbers, and email on a second line and save precious space for other valuable content. You don't need to write out the words address, phone, or email, as this will be obvious to your reader. However, you should reference whether a phone number is a home number or cell number like this: H: 212-555-1111 C: 917-444-5555.

2. **Modify margins.** You can recoup a great deal of valuable space by readjusting your margins. Microsoft Word often defaults to margins of one inch or more, but you can manually change your margin settings to something smaller. I don't recommend anything lower than .6 for top, bottom, and side margins, but making this adjustment can make a significant difference.

3. **Update your punctuation.** Many resumes I see still use 2 spaces following the period at the end of the sentence. If you took a typing class decades ago, this is how you were taught to do this. However, this rule has been modified due to the flexibility computers offer us in regards to character spacing and the new norm is to use one space following the period. Sometimes making these minor adjustments determines if a sentence falls on one line or two.

4. **Use numbers instead of words.** Generally, when writing a number that is less than ten, the protocol is to write out the number. But in resume writing (and blog posts), the numbers are often very important indicators of impact and it is best to use the numerical representation of the number. Rather

than writing "propelled sales to ten million dollars in just three years," try "propelled sales to $10M in just 3 years.". A side benefit is that by using the numerical representation, you will save valuable space.

5. **Eliminate articles.** In resume writing, the articles *the, a,* and *an* are understood. You can write, "managed $3M account" rather than, "managed a $3M account" and you can write, "led team tasked with creating first help desk" rather than, "led the team tasked with creating the first help desk." By eliminating these words, you save room for something else you need to say.

6. **Get rid of orphans.** Orphans represent single words that fall on a separate line in the resume. Review any sentences where this occurs to see if you can rephrase a sentence to eliminate the orphan and use space more constructively.

4 Ways to Source Keywords for Your Resume

Keywords for resumes refer to the buzzwords or search terms that recruiters and hiring managers are using to source candidates for their open positions. Keywords generally relate to skills that are specific to the job function, industry, or business environment. Keywords have become increasingly important in the past few years as more companies are relying on ATS or Applicant Tracking Systems to source candidates. ATS systems parse information on resumes that are uploaded to job boards and company websites and resumes are viewed (or not viewed) based on how closely the words in the resume match the job requirements or keywords that the hiring authority has chosen to search on. If a resume lacks the keywords that are part of this vetting process, the resume may never be seen by a hiring manager. The same may be true for Linked in profiles. Most recruiters and hiring managers search profiles based on keywords and will only view the profiles that match the keywords they have selected.

One strategy for creating a keyword-rich resume is to create a section on the resume (preferably following the summary or introductory section) that lists the appropriate keywords. The section can be labeled **Areas of Expertise, Core Strengths & Capabilities, or Core Competencies.** This writing strategy makes it easy for the human reader to understand your skills and allows the ATS systems to find relevant keywords in your resume.

So how should you go about finding the right keywords for your resumes? Here are four recommendations.

1. **Review job postings** – Look at job postings for positions for which you would consider applying. What skills are repeated across job descriptions in the requirements section? Use those words in your resume to build out your keyword section.

2. **Review keyword lists.** Wendy Enelow is the author of four books on keywords that you can find at www.wendyenelow.com. She has sourced 25,000 keywords and keyword phrases across 5,400 job positions and titles in 28 industries and professions.

3. **Use LinkedIn's skills section.** Go to your LinkedIn profile and click on the *more* tab to locate the skills section. Type a skill into the search box and a pull-down menu will appear with alternative skills that are similar to the one you typed in the search box. This can help you source additional keywords for your resume as well as your LinkedIn skills section.

4. **Use a resume optimization service.** See just how optimized your resume is for keywords by putting it through the same type of applicant tracking software tools used by employers to source candidates based on keyword searches. Preptel (www.preptel.com) is an example of a service that allows you to customize your resume and keywords for each position you are applying to by leveraging their tools that mirror the applicant tracking systems.

CHAPTER 3

5 Networking Lessons I Wish I'd Learned in High School: Advice on How to Strengthen the Quality of Your Network and Network More Strategically

Some people would rather go to the dentist than go to a networking meeting or event. Many avoid it altogether throughout their careers and find themselves in a bind when they are in a job search and aren't connected to anyone who can help. Flossing your teeth daily is proactive and preventative dental care. Networking on a regular basis is a proactive career management strategy that keeps you connected to people who can potentially influence and accelerate your job search. Neglect your teeth and you end up with a lot of pain and a huge dental bill. Neglect your network and you end up with an extended job search and months of lost income. This chapter offers tips for keeping your online and offline network healthy and strong.

Networking With a School or Corporate Alumni Connection

One of the best ways to foster a networking relationship is through a school or corporate alumni connection. Such connections are considered warm leads because a certain degree of relationship already exists. Warm leads are more viable than cold calls where no relationship is present. Members of the same affinity group are often more likely to help one another. But how do you approach people authentically, without making them feel uncomfortable with your request to meet with them and without making them feel they cannot meet your expectations for assistance? Here are some tips for building a quality relationship with alumni without asking for a favor or creating expectations that make the other person feel uncomfortable or unwilling to help.

1. **When you contact the person, remind them of the affinity relationship.** Alumni connections from schools and corporations are powerful affinity groups. Even if you didn't know the person during your time in school or tenure with a company, there is still generally a stronger bond between people who traveled in the same social and professional circles.

2. **Let the person know why you are interested in connecting with them.** Perhaps they are in the same profession or industry as you or they work for an organization you have identified as one of your target companies. State very clearly that you have no expectation that they can help you secure an interview. Let them know, however, that you have identified the company, profession, or industry as one you are interested in learning more about.

3. **Ask if they would be willing to speak with you** so you can learn more about the company, profession, or industry's culture. Stress that you don't expect them to give up a lot of their time and that you will make the meeting very brief.

4. **If the person agrees, plan for a 20 to 30 minute conversation** that includes a brief introduction of who you are and what your professional accomplishments and future goals are. Follow with an open Q&A about them. Ask questions about what they do professionally, what their role in the company is, and their thoughts about trends they see in the company, profession, and industry.

5. **Ask for recommendations regarding other people they suggest you talk to** or other ideas on how you might get closer to your professional goal. If you know of a particular opening at their company that you are interested in pursuing, ask what would be the best way to get closer to the decision maker (without asking them to refer you).

6. **Thank them for their time,** ask them if you can help them in any way, and offer to reciprocate information on a topic of interest to them.

7. **Create a strategy for staying in touch** periodically, either through a social or business networking tool or general emails or meetings if appropriate.

As the person gets to know you better, they may be willing to share information on contacts and even introduce you to some key decision makers. But keep in mind that networking is a process and it takes time to grow trusted relationships. Develop authentic relationships that position you as a giver rather than a taker and create consistent "touch points" with your network to build the relationship and keep it strong. The more trusted relationships you build and the more frequently you find legitimate ways to connect, the more likely you are to find people who can help you reach your career goals.

Barbara Safani

10 Tips for Helping Your Child Land His First Job Out of College

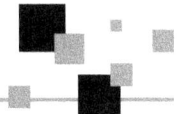

I find that many college students don't start learning about the job search process until they graduate, which in my opinion is at least four years too late. I'm noticing that many parents are feeling the stress as their children embark on their first job search in a challenging market. Here are my top ten tips for helping your child craft a career management strategy while they are still in college to increase their chances of landing a job swiftly after graduation.

1. **Work a minimum wage job during the academic school year.** I'm a firm believer that everyone should work at least one minimum wage job during their life. Flipping burgers, bagging groceries, running deliveries, or working a cash register are all jobs that help kids gain a comfort level dealing with people and working under fast-paced and often stressful conditions. These jobs teach humility, patience, and control and give kids a sense of independence. In addition, they will make them better appreciate the next job when it comes along. Juggling school and work efficiently also conveys a certain level of responsibility and maturity to prospective employers later on when the student is searching for a full-time role.

2. **Visit your college career services office early and often.** Most students show up in the college career services office once or twice and rarely before their senior year. A better strategy would be for the student to make an initial appointment freshman year and build a relationship with the counselors so they can guide him throughout his college career and keep him top of mind for appropriate internships. This may be the only time in your child's life when he will receive career counseling services at no additional charge as it is included in the college tuition.

3. **Get as many internships as you can as early as you can.** During the summer months and winter breaks, recommend sourcing an internship. If your child worked for pay during the school year, he may be able to go without the paycheck over the break and pick up some specific professional experience crunched into a 2 to 3 month break. If he has a strong interest in a particular industry, he can try to source something in that industry, but if not, he can shoot for an internship where he can pick up some general professional skills that he can repeat in other industry internships later on until he figures out his career aspirations.

4. **Source relevant volunteer opportunities.** This may include taking on a leadership role in a student chapter of a relevant professional organization or starting up an on campus club related to something your child is passionate about. Help him brainstorm activities that can supplement the college curriculum, showcase leadership skills, and provide opportunities to source important connections.

5. **Join LinkedIn.** Freshman year of college is not too early. Your child will already have some skills to add to the profile, maybe a job or two, and perhaps some volunteer or internship experience. For a student, it's better to have an abbreviated profile on LinkedIn than none at all. And by being a member, he can begin to search for people who may be able to help him decide on a future career direction and eventually land a job.

6. **Become findable.** It's easy for anyone these days to create a digital footprint without years of experience. Students can position themselves as subject matter experts or at least subject matter experts in training by showcasing their talents online. A journalism or English major could start a blog and link to articles or creative writing pieces. A finance major could blog about the financial markets. A theater major could post performance videos on YouTube. A history major could post a video explaining a particular historic event. The possibilities are endless.

7. **Show your kids how to source important connections.** Teach your child to be cognizant of who on campus may be an ally for him once he starts looking for a job. It may be his favorite economics professor, an alumni that came to the school to do a presentation, or a guest lecturer who presented on a topic that fascinates your child. Suggest he build relationships with upper classmen. By doing so, he will be able to learn from their experiences following graduation and benefit from their trial and error of what worked and didn't work during their job search.

8. **Encourage good grades… but not too good.** We all want our children to succeed academically, but it's important not to overemphasize the importance of grades over other critical career building and character building activities. The reality is that the only time an employer will ever care about your child's grades is the year he graduates from college. At that juncture, employers may view the GPA as an indicator of success in school, which may have some transferability to the world of work. Once your child applies for that second job out of school, few employers will care what his GPA was and will base his candidacy on success achieved in the previous job. So achieving a 4.0 while sacrificing opportunities to attain real life work skills and build authentic relationships with others is

not a sound career management strategy. Achieving a 4.0 doesn't make a student a better candidate and it may even work against the student as some employers will wonder what other important life experiences the student gave up in order to attain the exceptional GPA.

9. **Suggest an activity to improve public speaking.** Interviews can be daunting for seasoned professionals. They can be even harder for new graduates. A public speaking class, a job giving incoming student campus tours, or a role in an on-campus play can help students hone their public speaking skills and become more confident during interviews.

10. **Let go.** Be supportive, offer suggestions and recommendations, and introduce your child to contacts whenever possible. But set the expectation that this is your child's job search, your child's life, and another important step on his road to independence.

LinkedIn Tips

LinkedIn is a fantastic tool for connecting and reconnecting with business colleagues to accelerate your networking and your job search. It is an exceptionally robust platform, but few take full advantage of its capabilities. Here are some suggestions for getting the most out of LinkedIn.

1. **Create a keyword driven summary.** Forget about the summaries that describe you as passionate, a great communicator, and a team player. LinkedIn is all about searchability and recruiters and hiring managers don't search on those clichéd phrases. Instead, focus on the relevant keywords for your industry and job function and be sure to really build out the specialties section. Like resumes, no recruiter is really reading your LinkedIn profile. They are performing multiple sophisticated keyword searches looking for a match. Make every word count.

2. **Monitor your profile views.** Check the jobs tab regularly to see how many people have viewed your profile. If the number is exceptionally low, perhaps you need to tweak your profile to improve your searchability.

3. **Don't ignore the events listings.** Many hiring authorities search for top talent on LinkedIn by looking in the events section. They scour the list of events on LinkedIn to see who is attending certain industry events and often make connections directly through the events section rather than the user profile section.

4. **Spend time in the answers section.** Again, hiring managers are looking for the trendsetters and industry leaders. Often these people are participating in the answers section of LinkedIn, providing leadership and guidance, building credibility, and demonstrating authority.

5. **Include a picture.** People want to see whom they are doing business with. The picture starts solidifying the trust. The picture is part of your personal brand. Get over your insecurities about having the picture up on LinkedIn. It is here to stay and it is an important component in the relationship building process.

6. **Use features that help you track company information.** The companies tab on LinkedIn lets you track real-time movement within companies. This is an excellent way to be in the know about companies you are targeting.

7. **Don't worry about upgrading to the paid level of service.** This level is designed for recruiters and marketers, not job seekers. LinkedIn has an enormous amount of utility for job seekers at the free level of service.

8. **Pay attention to your privacy settings.** LinkedIn generally assumes you want a high level of privacy and will default to that setting unless you tell it otherwise. Everyone should review their settings and make sure they are aligned with your professional goals. For example, you can control who can tell that you have reviewed their profile. As a job seeker you will probably be researching multiple LinkedIn profiles, and you don't necessarily want everyone to know you are searching their profile. You can change this setting to anonymous.

9. **Ditch connections that don't make sense.** It is okay to terminate a connection with someone who you don't know and don't plan on building a relationship with. The degrees of separation work best when there is some affinity between you and the person you are connected to. Without that affinity, it will be more difficult to reach out to that person for an introduction to someone in their network.

10. **Keep learning about LinkedIn.** Take advantage of the LinkedIn Learning Center and the LinkedIn blog to get the most out of LinkedIn and stay on top of new features.

11. **Fill out the experience section completely.** Profiles that contain at least one past position in addition to a current position are seven times more likely to be viewed.

12. **Connect to at least 50 trusted colleagues.** According to sources at LinkedIn, fifty seems to be the "magic number" necessary to reach the critical mass that makes it easier to source second and third degree contacts.

13. **Try to get at least 3 recommendations in all areas of tip #13.** Every time you receive an endorsement, a message goes out to both your network and the network of the person who offered the endorsement. This is a great way to become top of mind with people quickly.

14. **Be strategic about your vanity url.** LinkedIn allows you to customize your url with your name. This makes it easier for people to find your profile and it helps with optimization efforts overall. When selecting a vanity url, the best strategy is to use your first name and last name with lower case letters and no spaces or dashes. If your name is already taken, the second best choice is to use your last name and first name with lower case letters and no spaces or dashes.

15. **Add volunteer experience to your profile.** A 2011 LinkedIn study showed that 20% of hiring managers considered relevant volunteer experience when making hiring decisions.

16. **Add skills.** This helps with optimization even more than the specialties section. If you click on the skills section under the "More" tab on the toolbar, you can key in a specific skill and get a list of related skills to help you build out your skills section. You can also view other profiles of people who have listed the same skill and see groups that are related to that particular skill set.

17. **Review company pages.** If you have your own company and add a company page on LinkedIn, it will be easier for people to find you in searches. If you are a job seeker, viewing company pages helps you find out who in your network works for that company. It also shows which people from your school alumni work at that company.

18. **Save job leads.** The jobs page allows you to save postings that you are interested in to make it easier to review them.

19. **Use LinkedIn Signals.** This feature, located in the "News" tab, lets you filter the information that is most important to you. You can click on the search all status updates button on the homepage and search on a particular topic such as "marketing jobs" or "JPMorgan Chase jobs" and source specific user status updates that relate to your search criteria.

20. **Be a stealth job seeker.** If you want to leverage LinkedIn for job leads but are currently employed and don't want your employer to become suspicious of your LinkedIn activity, customize your settings and turn off your activity broadcasts so you can connect discreetly. You can also hide your connections while you are looking so your boss can't see if you've connected to a competitor or you can hide information on your group activity for the same reason.

21. **Use LinkedIn Today to view trending topics.** On the LinkedIn homepage, you can view the articles that are most shared across LinkedIn, your professional community, and your connections and save relevant articles to be reviewed at a later time.

22. **Get on LinkedIn Mobile.** LinkedIn recently revamped their mobile apps making it easier for colleagues to connect on the go.

LinkedIn Invites: When a Potential Connection Quickly Becomes a Disconnect

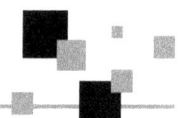

I receive many invitations on LinkedIn and while I am happy to accept most of them, sometimes the invite process is so poorly managed that the last thing I want to do is connect. Since I seem to see the same LinkedIn networking mistakes repeated over and over, I decided to post them here. Here are my top four.

1. **Not enough information.** I recently received an invitation from someone that read, "I would like to introduce myself." That was it. I searched their profile but all that was listed was company names, job titles, and employment dates. Please do not make me work so hard. Just give me the facts. Create a branded, detailed profile and explain to me what possible synergies we might have.

2. **Expecting too much too fast.** Sometimes I receive invitations from people asking me if I know of any job openings. I don't even know you yet. If you take the time to get to know me first and prove your value to an employer, I will certainly open up my network and help you if I can.

3. **Just plain laziness.** Frequently I receive invitations that were simply copied and pasted from a LinkedIn boilerplate template. How can you send me an invite that reads, "You are someone I know and trust" when I have never met you? Please respect me enough to send me a personalized invitation that explains why we should connect.

4. **Unwillingness to share.** Some people send me invitations to connect so they can mine my database, yet their contacts are protected. I think the concept of sharing was covered in kindergarten. If you have no intentions of creating a reciprocal relationship, don't bother sending me an invitation.

Here are some examples of alternative messaging that are more likely to result in an accepted invitation:

1. **Create common ground.** Hi! I noticed that you and I are affiliated with the same company and since you are a career strategist and I am a recruiter, I think there may be ways that we can help feed each other's pipeline. I'd love to learn more about what you do and share some information about my practice as well. Would love to connect.

2. **Start an authentic relationship.** Barbara...I decided to skip the boring LinkedIn template and just introduce myself to you. We are both in the business of helping people find better jobs and more fulfilling careers and I would be interested in sharing best practices with you. Do you have time to talk?

3. **Focus on the affinity.** I've recently been reviewing the profiles of people who have worked for the same companies as me and I came across your information. While I know we've never met, I've found that people who have worked for the same employer can often benefit from sharing information and experiences. Would you like to connect through LinkedIn?

4. **Give something before you expect to get something.** I see from your profile that you help people who are in a job search. I work with many clients who would benefit from your expertise. By connecting on LinkedIn, I can share more information about these clients with you.

Invest the few extra minutes to craft personalized and authentic messages to people you want to connect with. You will be glad that you did.

Status Update - I'm Still Looking for Work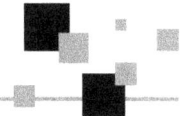

Lately I've been reading a lot of status updates on LinkedIn and Facebook that say things like "Project Manager professional looking for work" or "Looking for work in a tough economy" or "Just received my degree in accounting-looking for work." While I understand that these job seekers are trying to create visibility for their candidacy online, I don't recommend broadcasting this specific message in your status updates. Here's why:

1. **Blasting this message to your entire network makes you look desperate.** You might as well rent a billboard to promote your job search. Yes, I know there are stories about people landing a job this way, but these tactics get old very quickly.

2. **Posting this message makes people in your network uncomfortable.** Imagine agreeing to meet someone for coffee and before the coffee is even cool enough to drink you say, "I'm looking for work." It's awkward. It places an unrealistic expectation on your contact to come up with a solution for you. The same thing happens online when you post that you are looking for work.

3. **Sending this message leaves you little wiggle room for a follow up message.** Think about it. If you are still in the job search next week, what will your status update be? "Still looking for work," isn't going to cut it.

Status updates on business and social networking platforms are a way for you to build rapport and community and deepen the relationship with your contacts. Chose messages that showcase your expertise, share valuable information, give kudos to others, or broadcast an exciting endeavor you are working on (even if it is volunteer work). Here are some examples of alternative status updates you might want to adapt for your situation.

- **For a professional fundraiser:** Volunteering at the American Cancer Society Walkathon on Sunday; hope to raise more than $2M.

- **For an HR professional:** Attending a seminar on compensation plans for 2009 and beyond at (share the link)

- **For an advertising professional:** My colleague, John Smith just landed a major account with a leading luxury goods company. Way to go, John!

- **For a marketing student:** Just returned from a campus panel discussion on leveraging social media tools to build relationships with customers… fascinating!

- **For a CIO:** Reading an interesting article on new technologies in healthcare at (share the link)

- **For a Financial Analyst:** Boning up on study materials for the CFA Level II exam…looks like it's going to be a long night!

Create status updates that invite questions and further conversation, not ones that make your network run for cover. Remember, online networking, like traditional networking, is a process. Whenever possible, give before you get and you will be surprised how quickly you get something back in return.

Networking Your Way to Your Next Job

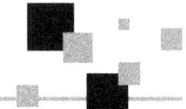

Most people land their jobs by building relationships with friends, family, colleagues, clients, or vendors that can introduce them to people who may be able to help them in their search. People are more likely to hire someone who comes recommended from a trusted source. Here are 22 tips for improving your networking strategy.

1. Networking is about asking for information, not asking for favors.

2. When requesting a networking meeting, always stress that you understand how busy the person is and that you just want to meet briefly.

3. When requesting a networking meeting, arrange everything on the other person's terms; time and location must be convenient for them.

4. While face-to-face networking is always best, graciously accept an opportunity to chat by phone if that is what's offered to you.

5. Work networking into your daily life — at your kid's soccer game, church, and even in line at the bank. Everyone is a potential connection.

6. When networking, expect to give more than you get, and soon you will be getting a lot.

7. Spend at least three-quarters of your job-search time networking for optimal results.

8. Find natural touch points like holidays and birthdays to reconnect with your network.

9. Networking is a lot of work, and if your networking is not working you may not be doing enough.

10. Reach out to affinity groups such as professional organizations, corporate or school alumni groups, and community groups to build a network.

11. Network with people who are different than you — older, younger, different ethnicities, different geographies, different industries, etc.

12. Create business cards with your name, contact information, and professional identity, and bring them with you wherever you go.

13. Add a signature line with your name and contact information to all of your e-mails to make you more memorable.

14. Write notes on the backs of business cards you receive at networking events to make each person more memorable.

15. You can't build a network overnight; try to build your network before you need it.

16. Create a list of companies you are interested in to share with people in your network; ask if they can refer you to anyone at these companies.

17. If you are uncomfortable networking in large groups, ask a more outgoing friend to accompany you.

18. To optimize networking events, go with a friend and network in different circles, then compare notes and leads at the end of the event.

19. Have a few meaningful conversations during networking events instead of trying to meet everyone to collect hundreds of business cards.

20. If you are shy, arrive at networking events early, when the setting is more intimate and the crowds aren't as overwhelming.

21. Ask people a lot of questions about themselves. People think you are a great conversationalist when you let them do most of the talking.

22. Don't pass on fee-based networking events in favor of free ones. Assess each opportunity based on the value you think it will offer.

Online Networking Tips for Job Search

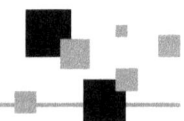

Online networking has revolutionized the way people build and maintain relationships and search for jobs. Imagine being able to go into the offices of everyone you know and search through their Rolodex or have a conversation with dozens of people from all over the world, all from the comfort of your keyboard. That is the power of online networking. Here are some tips on how to maximize your online presence, build meaningful relationships, and connect with people who may be able to help you in your search.

1. Create profiles on business and social networking and online identity sites to make it easier to be found by hiring managers.

2. With traditional networking, you can only be in one place at a time, but with online networking you can interact with multiple communities simultaneously.

3. Put your name in quotes into a search engine and see what comes back. Do you exist online and is your online presence distinctive?

4. Networking sites are not just for socializing; they are robust searchable databases full of critical information on people and companies.

5. Every online community has its own culture. Spend some time observing the culture before you jump in.

6. Nix the "I'm looking for work" status updates when chatting in online communities. They make you sound desperate and don't show your value.

7. Online networking does not have a "build it and they will come" mentality; work your online network daily.

8. Spend about an hour a day working your online network.

9. Hiring managers conduct online searches on candidates before the interview and may reject candidates based on what they do or do not find.

10. People who don't think online networking is relevant to their job search will become irrelevant to the hiring managers who think it is.

11. Add a professional headshot to your online profiles. When the photo is missing, people wonder why.

12. When inviting someone to your online network, be authentic and write a personal message. Nothing screams "lazy" like a canned invitation.

13. Take the time to create a robust profile on your networking sites; a complete profile is more searchable by recruiters and hiring managers.

14. Create a public profile with a vanity URL on your networking profiles, with your first and last name, to maximize your exposure.

15. Commit to adding at least five new contacts per week and reconnecting with at least five people in your network each week.

16. Reconnecting with someone you haven't spoken to in years by calling them is awkward; reconnecting through social media platforms is not.

17. Online networking is a great option for shy job seekers because unlike live networking, you can craft or edit a message before you hit send.

Do I Ever Think About You if We Aren't Connected Online?

My three closest friends don't participate in any form of social or business networking. You'll never find a business profile, status update, family photo, or even a poke from any of them on any online networking platform. While I ponder a "social media intervention," I continue to reach out to my friends on their terms, which includes email and phone contact and an annual snail mail holiday card. I have to admit; it's a lot more work to keep in touch this way and it takes more thought and planning on my part. But since these three friends mean the world to me, I try my best to stay in touch.

But what if I weren't as close to these people? Would I bother? Where's the threshold between making someone's life easy and too much work? What if you are a job seeker? During a search, you need a lot of contacts, both strong and weak networking links. Remaining top of mind with the weaker links is tough when you solely rely on email, a phone call, or a holiday card. With those limited means of communication and interaction, will your network bother to stay in touch? I often hear people complaining that social media is a frivolous waste of time. I disagree. I think it's a time saver and an efficient way to keep up with people and let them know what's going on in your world. This makes people feel connected. Feeling connected makes people more likely to offer help and advice.

I talked to one of my closest friends recently. It's been a long time since we spoke. Long enough for major events to occur in both our lives without the other one having a clue about it. I must admit that I was a bit sad when I realized that 300+ virtual friends know what I did last weekend and one of my dearest friends hasn't known what's been going on with me for much longer.

Imagine sending your resume to a recruiter and letting it sit in his database for years versus reaching out to recruiters on LinkedIn or Facebook to actively network with them. Think about the implications of sending a resume into the job board black hole versus building engagement with a company via their Facebook fan page.

Contemplate leaving a weak networking contact 10 unanswered voicemails versus including them in an online dialogue. Social networking works. Whether it's for maintaining friendships or managing your career.

World Trade Center Memories from the Bridge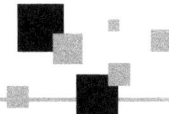

Many years ago, I worked in the World Financial Center, adjacent to the World Trade Center. Every morning, after getting off the subway at the WTC stop, I needed to walk across an indoor bridge that connected the WTC to my office. The bridge always seemed endless and it often reminded me of that poppy field that Dorothy had to cross before getting to The Emerald City.

People were always walking at a fast pace across that bridge because that's what New Yorkers do and because we were all trying to get to our offices before 9am. Sometimes I would spot colleagues on the bridge and we would walk across together. The length of the bridge was such that it allowed you to have enough of a conversation with the other person to learn something new about them. Sometimes it was an update on their weekend or their personal life. Other times it was a glimpse into their childhood or a sliver of information about their future hopes and dreams. At the time, it seemed like I was just chitchatting and trying to stay occupied while crossing the bridge. However, the reality was that I was actually networking... sharing information with colleagues that helped deepen the relationship and build trust and rapport.

I left that job several years before 9/11 and lost touch with many of my "bridge buddies." Not long after 9/11, I was doing some consulting work downtown in another one of the World Financial Center buildings. But this time the bridge was gone. A makeshift bridge made of steel provided an interim solution for those who needed to trek across. No longer an enclosed bridge, the new bridge was ugly, scary, and raw and it did nothing to shield me from the cold winter elements. Being down at Ground Zero was certainly an emotional experience. Walking across that bridge, freezing and alone was my own personal moment of loss.

That's when I realized how important it was to stay connected to people from my past. That's when I realized that those chats on the bridge were really much more than small talk. I don't remember a lot of the projects I worked on with these colleagues or what we talked about at work. But I remember the conversations on the bridge in vivid detail because they weren't about work; they were about the person...and knowing something about the person is what builds the connection. It's as if the physical bridge gave me the opportunity to cross the relationship bridge between work colleague and friend.

I've reconnected with some of my friends from the bridge. I think of them frequently, but I always think of them on 9/11. What's your bridge between work colleague and friend? Maybe it's the company cafeteria, the bar across the street, or some other hangout. Find the bridge, nurture it, and never let it disappear.

Creepy Networking

Despite all the information available about "netiquette" and the importance of networking strategically online, I continue to get dozens of mystery online networking requests. Sometimes the connection is as weak as being a member of the same group (with 50,000 other members) or as bizarre as asking for a face-to-face meeting based on the fact that we reside in the same city.

Something strange seems to happen to some people when they network online. It's as if some people think that none of the common rules for building relationships exist. Could you imagine ever saying any of the following things over the phone or in person to someone you don't know?

1. I've seen you walking down this block in the neighborhood before. Want to meet for coffee?

2. Someone told me we used to work for the same company that employs 20,000 people. Want to chat sometime?

3. I found your number in the phone book. Maybe we have something in common.

4. I heard through the grapevine that you work for a company where I would really like to work. Can you tell me more about what it's like to work there?

5. I found you in the 1997 student alumni directory. I'm a graduate of the class of 1980. Would you like to compare notes?

6. I know I've never actually met you before and you have no idea who I am. But someone suggested I say, "Since you are someone I know and trust, I would like to add you to my network." Does that work for you? (Hint: that's verbatim from a LinkedIn template that people seem to use whether they know you or not).

7. You looked like someone I should know, so I followed you home, made note of your address and then did a search to find your phone number. Would love to meet formally sometime.

8. I found your name and number written on a cocktail napkin at a local restaurant and I decided to call you. I figured, what do I have to lose?

Of course, you wouldn't say any of these things! So why do people think this approach will work online? If you are using LinkedIn or other social media tools to connect with others, create authentic relationships and recognize that the affinity will grow over time. Even on Twitter where there are generally no gatekeepers for connecting with others, it's still advisable to follow the person for awhile and create a supportive and non-threatening dialogue before bringing the relationship face to face.

I am a fairly open connector on LinkedIn as well as other social media platforms. But I have to know a little bit about you and why you want to connect before I accept. Isn't that just common sense?

Networking Basics

1. **Ask for information rather than a job.** When you ask someone if they know if anyone is hiring, there is a simple yes/no response (usually no) which leaves the conversation at a standstill. Instead of asking about job openings, ask your contacts if they would be willing to talk to you to share information - about an industry, a company, a recruiter or whatever else will help get you one step closer to the ultimate hiring manager. Asking for a job can make the other person feel uncomfortable; asking for information can be flattering.

2. **Get on LinkedIn.** With 170M+ users, LinkedIn has become a "must have" resource for recruiters searching for top talent. If you aren't on LinkedIn, recruiters may come to the conclusion that you are not current, not serious, or not good enough at what you do to be in the running for their openings.

3. **Be on-message.** Prepare a succinct, compelling pitch about what you are looking for and why you are qualified. Keep this message consistent in your resume, your online profiles, and your conversations.

4. **Reach out to companies directly.** Do you dream of working for Google, Starbucks, JPMorgan Chase, or the Red Cross? If so, let the employer know that. More and more companies are filling positions through employee referrals and social networking and many never even post their open positions. Become an insider by reaching out to companies and expressing your interest before they have a job opening. If you can become top of mind with them, you increase the likelihood of being considered

should a position become available, or better still, of having a position created for you based on the outstanding value the employer thinks you could bring to the organization.

Why Networking Gets a Bad Rap and What to Do About It

Many people think that networking during a job search means calling everyone you know and asking them for a job. They associate networking with being pushy, overbearing, and an overall pest. People often shy away from networking because they don't want to be labeled as this type of person. However, research shows that 70-80 percent of all jobs are filled through networking. How can this be so, if networkers are such an annoying, self-serving lot?

Successful networkers are not egocentric, aggressive jerks. They show a sincere interest in their networking contacts. They work hard to develop a relationship, establish their credibility, and share information. They follow the rules of the game where everyone has something to gain. Like the lottery, you have to be in it to win it. Below are seven tips to follow for successful networking.

1. Don't ask for a job... ask for information.

Networking is not about asking everyone you know for a job. In fact, when you network you should never ask someone for a job. You ask them for information that will help you in your search. Your goal is to build a relationship and establish rapport so that if a potential opportunity becomes available in the future, they will want to refer you. Compare these two scenarios:

Scenario One

"Joe, I've been out of work for six months and I'm really strapped for cash. Do you know of any open positions in your department?"

You've put Joe in a very difficult position. Sure, he can sympathize with your situation, but he may not be able to offer you a job. Perhaps he's not in a position to refer you, or there's a hiring freeze, or there aren't any openings right now. Whatever answer Joe gives you, it's bound to be disappointing. So, to redeem himself, Joe says, "I don't know of any open positions, but why don't you give me your resume and I'll send it to the HR department where I work." Bad move. Unless your skills match a specific opening in the company at that point in time, it's bound to never be looked at. Joe will feel that he's done what he can for you, but you will be no better off.

Scenario Two

"Joe, as you know, I most recently worked for a medical device company in their marketing group. I know that you've been in pharmaceutical sales for the past 15 years and I'm very interested in learning more about marketing roles within your industry. I don't expect you to know of any open positions in your organization, but I'd like the opportunity to speak with you briefly to learn more about your organization and the pharmaceutical industry in general."

Joe may think, "Okay, here's a friend that wants some information and sees me as some sort of expert on the topic. That's kind of flattering. I guess I could spend a few minutes with him." Does Joe know you're looking for a job? Probably. But you are not asking him for a job; you're just asking him for advice and insight. The stakes are low and the expectations are reasonable, so he is more likely to help you.

2. Don't take up too much of the other person's time.

Have an agenda and keep the meeting on track. Nothing scares people more than the prospect of someone eating up a lot of their time. Many people don't want to cram yet another meeting into their already jam-packed day. Contrast these two situations:

Scenario One

You meet with Mary after a mutual friend has agreed to help you set up a brief 20-minute meeting. You neglect to prepare for the meeting, ramble, get off topic and spend an hour and a half with her. Mary feels that you have abused the use of her time and you haven't gotten to the critical questions you'd hoped to ask during the meeting. Mary feels burned and vows never to network again.

Scenario Two

You walk into the meeting with a prepared mental agenda that includes:

* A reminder of who referred you and perhaps some brief chitchat about that mutual acquaintance.
* A statement that you have no reason to believe Mary can offer you a position.
* An explanation of your agenda. "Today I'd like to tell you a bit about myself and get your perspective on the future of the high-tech industry." Remember to discuss your skills and accomplishments and show how you can add value to an organization.

By planning out your meeting ahead of time, you establish your professionalism, gain credibility, and cover all the critical agenda items.

3. Give the other person a chance to speak. Ask questions.

When you network, it is imperative that you do not do all the talking. If you have asked another person for advice, make sure they have the opportunity to offer it. Also, when you do all the talking, the other person might feel confused and unsure of what they are supposed to do with the information you have supplied. Here are some questions you can ask to keep your exchange balanced and establish rapport.

* How long have you been with this company/field?
* What do you like/dislike about your job?
* What type of training do you need for positions such as yours?
* What is the culture of this company and what are its guiding principles?

4. Ask for suggestions on how to expand your network.

One of the main goals of networking is to tap into the network of people you are meeting with. Each person you meet probably knows 200 or more people. If you can gain introductions to some of them, you quickly increase your network and your chances of finding the right connection. Ask your contacts if they can recommend a professional organization or the names of some other people you should be talking to.

5. Create a vehicle for follow-up.

If you want to establish rapport with another person, you need to create ways to keep the relationship going. Ask the person if you may keep them informed of your search progress. If you read an article that pertains to a discussion you had at a networking meeting, cut it out and send it to them with a brief note. Try to find at least two to three opportunities per year to reconnect with members of your network.

6. Find ways to reciprocate.

Building a network is about creating a genuine, caring relationship. Thank your contact for the information they have supplied and see if you can help them in some way. Maybe your contact is interested in living in an area that you are familiar with or has a child interested in attending the same school where you graduated. Share your knowledge of the school and your experience there as a way to help the other person. Keep notes on what you learn about your contacts so that future correspondence can have a personalized touch like, "How was Jane's first year of school?"

7. Send a thank you letter.

Always thank your contacts in person and follow up with a letter. If your handwriting is legible, the personalized touch is always appreciated.

Networking is an ongoing process. It requires persistence, attention, organization, and good will. Incorporate the art of networking into your job-search campaign now, and you will gain opportunities and build relationships that will last a lifetime.

Holiday Networking Can Facilitate New Year Opportunities

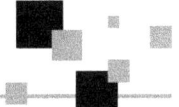

The holidays provide a natural touch point for reaching out to your network and seeing how friends, family, and colleagues are doing. It's also an excellent way to become top of mind with people in your network and open up a dialogue in the New Year. Here are some other things you can do during the holiday season to beef up your network and start meaningful career conversations in the New Year.

1. **Attend holiday parties.** Many professional associations host holiday parties. This is a great way to meet others in your field who may be able to make meaningful introductions for you.

2. **Throw your own party.** Have an intimate dinner party or a bigger bash at your home or nearby restaurant. This is a great way to practice your pitch and reconnect with people who may be able to assist you in your search.

3. **Ask for informational interviews.** The last two weeks of December are traditionally slow for most businesses. You may find that the decision makers who are in the office during those last two weeks are more likely to take a meeting with you.

4. **Volunteer.** Tis the season! Volunteer to do something meaningful in your personal or professional communities during December. Doing so can increase your visibility and jump-start some conversations with people who may be able to help you in the New Year.

5. **Take a vacation.** What better way to meet new decision makers? It doesn't need to be extravagant, just find new people to have conversations with. Let them know what you do and ask for their suggestions for expanding your brand's reach in a very informational, non-threatening way. You may just pick up a lead or two.

6. **Reconnect with friends of "Christmas Past".** Check out LinkedIn and Facebook and search for old friends. What better time to reconnect than the holiday season? Get over the fact that it's been awhile since you last spoke and take the first step. You may be pleasantly surprised by the response you get.

7. **Send holiday cards.** Holiday cards provide a natural "touch point" or opportunity to reconnect with friends, family, and colleagues. Reach out to your network now with some "best wishes" and holiday cheer and you will have a natural entrée into a job-related conversation in the New Year.

5 Networking Lessons I Wish I'd Learned in High School

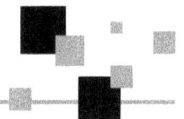

Recently I attended my high school reunion. It was great to see old friends, but one of the things that struck me was how many people I never got to know in high school. For many, the high school years are often tough ones, defined by insecurities and confusion. Kids often create their own social hierarchies in order to survive. Most teens aren't mature enough to understand the nuances of networking effectively and they miss opportunities to build certain relationships during their high school years. Unfortunately, as many of us age, we hang on to our high school insecurities and fail to nurture a robust and lasting network of people to reach out to as we build our professional lives. Here are my five suggestions for breaking out of the high school mentality in an effort to achieve your professional goals and move towards a stronger professional network.

1. **Eat lunch at a different table each day.** In high school, students tended to share their lunch hour with the same group of kids day in and day out. I often see adults in the corporate world do the same thing. Don't go to lunch with the same person every day. Expand your network by reaching out to others in your department or division. Spend time with people in peripheral

departments with professional agendas that are different from yours. Lunchtime is a great time to get to know someone on a more personal level. People who take the time to build strong personal relationships have stronger networks to reach out to when they need assistance.

2. **Touch the "untouchables."** When I was in high school, there were several cliques. It could be very hard to break into a clique if you weren't part of the activity, such as sports or theater, that fueled the clique. Adults often think that certain people on the corporate ladder are untouchable, that they can't approach a C-suite executive or a potential contact in a new industry they are interested in penetrating. They assume they won't give them the time of day. While some won't, others will. You won't know until you approach them.

3. **Stop thinking that everything is about you.** High school students often obsess about themselves and everything that is going on in their life. Small defeats seem like major ones and many teens are convinced that everyone is watching their every move and waiting for them to slip up. Sometimes we carry this "me-centric" way of thinking into our professional lives. Usually people aren't paying nearly as much attention to you as you think they are. However, they will pay attention to how you interact with them. So when you network, stop thinking about yourself and what you need and start thinking about how you can help another person. Give to give, and if you get something in return, consider it gravy. Chances are good that if you position yourself as someone who tries to help others, the reciprocity will follow.

4. **Interact with people who are not just like you.** In my high school, it was sometimes tough to interact with students in different grades. A junior generally didn't hang out with a freshman and you rarely saw a sophomore dating a senior. Friendships across racial and ethnic lines occurred, but probably not as frequently as they could have. This phenomenon happens with adults all the time. People often limit their networks to contacts in the same job function, industry, or professional level. Older professionals reach out to their younger colleagues with less frequency, and networks aren't always as racially integrated as they should be. To improve the quality of your network, diversify. Be all inclusive and reach out to people of all ages, professions, and backgrounds.

5. **Have a life outside of high school.** When I was a teen, most of my social life centered around high school. It wasn't until I was a senior and got my first "real job" that I started interacting with people I didn't know from school. Most of them were high school students as well and most of them went to

the same school, but I never would have met them if I didn't have this job. For various reasons, our paths just never would have crossed. This part-time job was perhaps the richest experience of all my high school years. It taught me that my life could be enriched by people that were outside of my usual inner circle. Adults sometimes become enmeshed in the culture of their companies and forget that there is a whole world of professionals to tap into. If their position is downsized, they struggle because all their connections are with people in the company that just let them go. To better manage your career, find other communities that support your professional goals. Consider joining a professional association for your job function or industry to connect with others and build your network.

What insecurities or bad habits are holding you back from being a more effective networker? What can you do to change your strategy moving forward?

Volunteering as a Career Management Strategy

Helping out a community or cause that you are passionate about helps you build new skills and visibility that can enhance your professional credibility and open doors that can accelerate a career or a job search. Here are just a few of the fringe benefits that come with volunteer service.

- **Community.** Volunteering in a professional organization or other association that you care about brings you together with people who share similar interests or values. This common bond helps build relationships and trust. People are much more willing to share information with people who are part of their community because there is already a connection to that person.

- **Leadership.** Taking on a leadership role in an organization allows you to showcase your ability to direct others and think strategically about a process or project. If you can successfully lead a team or project in a volunteer environment, people in that community will notice and will act as advocates for you when other opportunities to lead surface.

- **Skill Development.** Through volunteer opportunities, you can begin to hone skills that may not be part of your current area of expertise but could be important to your future professional development. Skills acquired through a volunteer opportunity are no less valuable than those acquired through a paid opportunity, and the skills you build through a volunteer experience could help position you for a paid opportunity down the road.

- **Networking.** Informal conversations about companies and job leads go on all the time in volunteer-based personal and professional organizations and affinity groups. Some of the best assignments are routinely communicated through people, not job boards or search firms.

Like any other type of relationship you build, approach volunteer relationships with a "give to give" rather than a "give to get" attitude. You will be helping others and generating some good karma, but in the long run you will probably be quite pleased with the "return on investment" of your volunteer efforts.

In Networking, Sometimes a Conversation about Nothing is Something

Probably the biggest complaint I hear from job seekers about networking tools like Facebook and Twitter is that most people write about nothing. Following someone who writes about nothing is a waste of time. However, is a conversation about nothing really nothing or can it sometimes turn into something?

Real conversations are not always about something. No one is deep and profound 24/7. People have conversations to connect and interact with those around them. They use conversations to engage. Small talk about the weather, a new coffee house, a great sale, or a silly thing your kid just did is all part of the rhythm of a conversation. That's how relationships are built. So why do we assume that an online conversation isn't worth having unless someone says something meaningful?

Tweets and Facebook status updates are touch points. They are a window into how a person is feeling and how their day is going. They keep you top of mind with people in your life and can even interest people who don't know you well.

Here are a few silly, meaningless status updates from my Facebook page that recently sparked conversations:

1. Helped my son clean out his locker at school today...let's just say I wish I had been wearing gloves.

2. Two kids, 6 finals, 3 days, infinite drama

3. Wishing I could outsource my inbox

4. So now I know why the airlines charge $15 to check your bag-so that when they put it on the wrong flight, they have the funds to UPS it to your house the next day. Sheesh!

Different people chimed in on different posts for different reasons. Some were friends, others were colleagues, and others were clients. It didn't really matter how we were originally connected. For each message, there was someone out there that could relate to what I was posting and chose to respond. And that give and take, that sharing of information, that reciprocity, and that ability to empathize with another person is what builds a relationship. Relationships built on shared experiences build trust. People share information with people they trust. All types of information... including job leads. No interaction is meaningless if it helps support the relationship.

Of course, I'm not advocating that all your posts should be about nothing and it's equally important to give useful information to your network. I'm just saying that the posts about nothing may mean something to someone and might be the springboard for a great relationship.

Ideas for Face-to-Face Networking

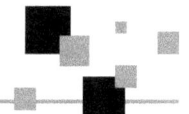

Affinity groups offer some of the best opportunities for networking for a job search because the original bond was created based on the common connection, interest or hobby, not the fact that you are looking for a job. Affinity groups allow you to develop trust and rapport before moving on to the subject of the job search. If trust has been previously established, it's much easier to start a conversation about your job search without having it look like you are asking for a favor. Here are a few more offline affinity groups worth exploring.

- **The PTA.** Members of parent groups are passionate advocates for their children's education. Affinity groups fueled by passion create members with strong bonds, and members of groups such as these are more likely to help others because of their strong sense of community and connection.

- **Local house of worship.** Religion is an immediate connector for many people. A church, synagogue, or mosque represents the ultimate community for many and members are very likely to help others in their time of need.

- **The train or bus.** In many communities, people take the same method of transportation at the same time every day and they see the same people. These people often form relationships simply because they happen to commute together. These same people may be excellent resources for job leads.

- **The porch or lobby.** I've started a lot of great conversations with people while waiting for the elevator in my lobby. My homeowner friends start conversations by sitting on their porches and chatting with the neighbors who are nearby.

- **The line at the post office, motor vehicles, and the supermarket checkout.** It happens. Many people report making new connections with strangers solely because they both happened to be stuck on the same line at the same time. You never know!

Tips for Building Visibility at Professional Development Meetings

Attending a professional development meeting in the near future? Here are some suggestions for getting the most out of the event.

- Show up at events early so you can meet the speaker. It's easier to build rapport before the presentation, when there are less people vying for the speaker's attention. Follow-up with an email or card thanking the speaker for spending time with you prior to the presentation.

- Ask a question during the Q&A portion of the presentation. State your name and a brief one-liner about yourself before stating your question. This allows you to introduce yourself to everyone in the room and increase the likelihood that people will seek you out for a conversation later.

- Thank the organizers before you leave. This is a nice gesture and a good way to build rapport with people who are close to the organization's membership. Perhaps you'll uncover an opportunity for you to assist with a future event and gain greater access to membership contacts.

The Healing Power of Social Networking

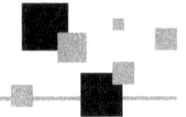

Many articles have been written about what people perceive as the awkwardness of having someone from your junior high or high school days, who you haven't talked to in decades, find you and ask to friend you on Facebook. I have an entirely different take on this and here's why.

A few years ago, I started a networking group on Facebook to reconnect with some old friends from high school. Initially, my boomer friends were skeptical and even a little bit nervous about joining, but many did so, perhaps to humor me or maybe just because they were curious or wanted to friend their children to see what they were up to online.

What started out as a very modest sized group has grown to the hundreds, thanks to some very tenacious Facebook users and some core friends with a killer email list and super human cyber sleuthing capabilities. While it's fascinating to see the numbers in the group grow each day, what's more amazing is the healing power of the group.

Let's face it…high school is not exactly the easiest time in life and the relationships formed there are filled with excitement, passion, disappointment, embarrassment, and defeat.

Yet despite all that, the affinity within the group is quite powerful. The ties you form with your high school peers are tough to match, even if you weren't voted "best athlete" or "most likely to succeed." With those ties comes the power to forgive. Since starting the group, friends have told me about some amazing things that have happened to them online. Two of my friends told me about friendships that blew up in high school or soon after and were never revisited again…until Facebook. Facebook gave them the courage to say, "So what was that argument all about and who cares anymore?" Another friend told me he hardly remembers anyone from high school (he cut many classes), yet despite what he initially thought, his wall is full of friends, friends of friends, jokes, videos, old photos, etc.

So if someone from your past reaches out to you on a social or business networking site, don't make your decision to accept the invitation based solely on what the relationship was so many years ago…instead, base your decision on what the relationship could be.

Top Excuses for Not Networking

The idea of networking is often resisted by job seekers. Since a strong network is the key to a successful job search, it's important to uncover the reasons for this resistance. Here are the most common obstacles people face and some recommendations for how to move past them.

1. Not wanting to ask for a favor

Many people think that when you network you are asking someone for a job. This is not the goal of networking. When you network, you never ask for a job. You ask for information about an industry, company, or position.

2. Fear of rejection

Many people fear that if they ask for information, the other person might not be willing to talk to them. While it is true that not everyone will agree to meet with you, many people will extend help to you and you have nothing to lose by asking.

3. Lack of awareness regarding the effectiveness of networking

Most people in a job search spend too much time canvassing the open job market, the market everyone gets to see through job posting boards and recruiters. Far fewer explore the hidden market; the jobs that are never posted, but instead are filled through connections. The odds of finding a position through the smaller, hidden market are greater than those in the open market.

4. Not comfortable talking to people they don't know

60% of the population considers themselves shy. This perception leads to less networking. If the prospect of speaking to someone you don't know is overwhelming right now, start to build your network by talking with people you do know such as friends, family, neighbors, or your doctor or dentist. If they can lead you to others who can help you gain necessary information for your search, your network will grow in a steady, comfortable way.

5. Wanting to do it all on your own

When you are selected for a position, it's because you have the skills to support the needs of the position. You showcase your individual accomplishments and differentiate yourself from the competition. However, in order to tell your stories to the right person, you need to cast a wide net. You leverage your network to find the right audience, not to get the job.

6. Uncomfortable talking about yourself

Many of us were raised to be humble and not to brag. Networking and interviewing requires that you talk about yourself and your accomplishments. When you talk about your skills, you are not bragging. It's only bragging if your discussion contains hyperbole, half truths, or lies.

7. Concerns about others knowing your business

Feeling too proud to tell people you are in a job search? Examine the cause. Have you assumed that networking is asking for a job? Next, examine the consequences. If you fail to incorporate networking as a method of search, it may take you much longer to find a job.

8. Lack of knowledge regarding the process

If you don't understand networking, now's the time to learn. To be an effective networker, you need to be willing to share information, build relationships based on trust and reciprocity, leverage existing relationships to create new ones, and create ways to stay in touch to continue giving. Those who don't understand the process, who use people for information and never build the relationship or return the favor, give networking a bad name and lose credibility in the eyes of others.

9. Expecting things to move too quickly

Networking is an ongoing process. Like a child, your network needs time to grow and you need to nurture it along the way. You must pay attention to your network to keep relationships strong. Many contacts are not able to lead you to the person capable of making a hiring decision. You must constantly "stir the pot" to effectively network. Take care of your network and it will in turn take care of you.

Accelerate Your Networking during the Slow Summer Months

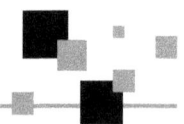

When I counsel clients on their job search during the summer months, they often tell me that they plan to put their search on hold because they think that everyone is out of town and no one is hiring during this season.

Actually, the summer months can be the best time to step up your search campaign because so many applicants believe this misperception of the market. Consider the following:

Fewer people in town could mean more opportunity.

Savvy job seekers know that the more visible they are, the greater the chances of meeting the person that can connect them with a viable job opportunity. This concept may be even more important when you are searching during the summer months. Some job seekers make the mistake of taking a break from their search during the summer months because they assume that no one is in the hiring mode. The reality is that summer networking may be more productive. Decision makers' schedules are not as tight and they may be more generous with their time. By establishing relationships with the key players now, you are more likely to be remembered when the hiring picks up.

People do more entertaining during the summer months.

Memorial Day weekend is synonymous with firing up the grill, taking the tarp off the pool, and planning informal gatherings. These venues are excellent opportunities to reconnect with old friends and hook up with new contacts. There is always a chance to share information about what you do at these events.

Networking options increase in the warm summer months.

With the warm weather comes the opportunity to network in places that you can't network in the colder months. One such place is the golf course. Golf continues to be one of the most effective places for referrals and new business. If you have children, consider spending time with them in the playground. Parks are filled with people who have connections to others. Parents tend to gravitate to certain playgrounds on a regular basis, so you have a chance to establish and grow the relationship over several visits. Bring along toys that encourage cooperative play including balls, Frisbees, and jump ropes and you'll have an audience of eager kids and adults in no time.

Family obligations may be reduced during summer.

If you have older children, your family obligations might be reduced during the summer months. Children typically aren't juggling as many activities and their time away from you may be extended if they are in a day or sleep away camp program. This could be the perfect time to participate in some early morning or after hours meetings and activities that are difficult to commit to during the school year.

Establishing relationships in the summer time is an excellent way to make inroads with decision makers who may be hiring in the fall. Hiring managers may be more accessible, more relaxed, and just in a better frame of mind during the summer months.

Make Your Network Work for You

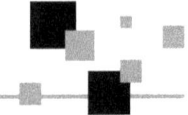

Networking is the art of building and maintaining mutually beneficial relationships. Frequently, when I coach people who are in a job search and we discuss networking within the context of a job search, many will say, "Does that really work?" Like anything else, networking requires a bit of practice and finesse, but if done correctly, networking can be an invaluable part of your job search campaign. Here are a few tips to help you develop a network that works for you.

Be a teacher

Not everyone you meet will understand what networking is or how they can help you. Many think that the best way they can help a job seeker is to take their resume and pass it on to their human resource department. While their intentions are noble, their strategy is seriously flawed. HR managers, like recruiters, may only be motivated to take action on your resume if there is a current job opening within the organization that matches your skills. If a position is not available, they have no incentive to contact you and the connection is lost. Rather than giving your contacts a resume, thank them but tell them that what you would really like is an introduction to someone at that company so you can learn more about the company, share information about yourself, and begin to build a relationship.

Be a helper

Good networking is all about reciprocity. Always try to give more than you receive. Perhaps you have information about a particular company, industry, or educational program that would be valuable to someone in your network. Look for ways to help people in your network achieve their goals and they will be more likely to help you in return.

Be a conduit

Become a great connector for people and open up your network to them. Always think about who you might know that could help other people in your network in some way.

Be patient

People may want to help you, but you may not be the first item on their agenda. If someone agrees to meet with you, but can't do so immediately, accept the offer graciously.

Be authentic

Take a sincere interest in the lives of the people you meet. Don't milk people for information and then abandon the relationship. Nobody wants to feel like they are being taken advantage of. Find ways to reconnect with your network periodically to stay up to date and let them know that you care about what is going on in.

I Just Landed a New Job So I'm Done Networking, Right?

After you find a new position, the relationships you developed during your search may continue to be important to your career. Here are a few suggestions for maintaining a viable network once you conclude your job search.

Update contact information

Be sure to send information on your new work location to all those who supported your efforts. This includes all personal contacts, recruiters, and other interested parties. Thank them all for their efforts and support. LinkedIn and Facebook are great tools for keeping your network up to date.

Stay connected to colleagues

Keep in touch with co-workers, clients, and vendors from your previous position. By proactively managing these relationships now, you strengthen the quality of your network and improve the opportunity to leverage these relationships at another point in time. Keep in mind that reciprocity is an important piece of the networking dynamic and by staying in touch, you may be in a position to help your contacts should they decide to pursue other employment opportunities.

Keep professional memberships active

Continue to remain active in professional organizations. Contribute your time and knowledge to the organization's events, special interest groups, and newsletters. The visibility you create now will benefit your professional development in many ways. An excellent resource for finding appropriate professional organizations for your industry is weddles.com.

Conduct informational interviews

Remember how grateful you were when you were granted an informational interview or networking meeting? Consider doing the same if you are asked to offer advice or information to someone interested in your field or organization. What goes around comes around and such interviews give you the opportunity to source new talent, mentor a colleague, or build a relationship that will benefit both of you in the future.

Go to lunch

The lunch hour is a great time to bond with new co-workers and grow your network. Dine with a diverse group of colleagues across business units and job functions.

Networking: Mind Your Manners

Last month I had an absolutely delightful networking meeting with someone I met through a professional association. What made the meeting so memorable was that the person I was networking with did everything right. She followed every rule of networking including:

1. Being flexible with the meeting time and location and asking me what was convenient for me.

2. Telling me that she didn't want to take up too much of my time but wanted to touch base briefly.

3. Coming prepared to explain her value proposition and what she is looking to achieve in her job search.

4. Asking me what recommendations I had for other people she could talk to in the industry.

5. Practicing reciprocity by asking how she could help me achieve my professional goals.

6. Thanking me for my time.

I was thinking about this contact yesterday after having two back to back unpleasant networking experiences. In one situation, the networker had a very narrow and inconvenient window of time when she could meet. After I agreed to meet on her terms, I followed up with her the day before the meeting to confirm only to find out that she had to cancel.

In another situation, someone approached me through a distant contact on LinkedIn and asked to speak to me by phone to ask some career questions. We set a time, yet when I called her, I got her voicemail and still had not heard from her 24 hours later. Unfortunately, bad networking happens much too frequently and the people who abuse the concept of networking sometimes make it more difficult for those with good intentions to secure meetings.

The networker that got it right is on my A list. She is top of mind. If I can make an introduction for her or give her a job lead, I certainly will. As for the others, I will give them another chance to reach out to me, but the relationship has already been compromised and it will take some rebuilding on their part to repair.

5 Ways to Use Facebook for Your Job Search

Most people I talk to really enjoy Facebook's interface and spend at least a little bit of time there each day. Most acknowledge its benefits for keeping in touch with friends and family, but few recognize Facebook's implications for during a job search and its growing relevance as a job search and career management tool. With over 850 million users (a network that is approximately eight times larger than LinkedIn) and a robust demographic of professionals with 10+ years of work experience, the potential to connect with a key business contact via Facebook is enormous. Here are 5 tips for optimizing your job search strategy on Facebook.

1. **Like Pages** – Most major employers have company pages and many even have separate pages with information about careers at the company. By viewing these pages, you can learn a great deal about a company's culture and products and their open positions. Just use the search box on Facebook to find some the companies you are targeting in your search. By "liking" the page, you can start engaging in the conversations by commenting on the company page and you can also learn more about potential opportunities.

2. **Use Job Search Applications** – BranchOut, BeKnown, and Glassdoor Inside Connections are third party applications that run on the Facebook platform and allow you to connect with recruiters and people from companies

you are interested in without sharing all your personal information on Facebook. These applications leverage Facebook's huge network to help you connect with people who may be able to make important introductions for you.

3. **Subscribe** – What if you found someone who was a thought leader in your industry or someone who you wanted to get regular updates from but you don't really know them? By subscribing to their Facebook updates, you can receive their updates in your feed without friending them and they will be notified that you are a subscriber. Just key in their name in the search box, go to their profile, and click on subscribe if they have enabled this feature on their page. This is a great way to get on their radar and possibly turn a cold lead into a warm one.

4. **Use Timeline** – The new timeline profile is great for customizing your Facebook page and building your professional and personal brand. Important events and pictures can be highlighted, the pages you like can be prominently displayed, and you can show other interests such as the books you read or the music you like. Timeline is like your visual resume and it gives you many opportunities for building a compelling and engaging message of value.

5. **Create Engaging Status Updates** – Use your status updates to let your network know about professional events you are attending, interesting articles and books you are reading, and volunteer work you are doing to support your professional community. Write about companies and leaders you admire, share industry best practices, and give shout-outs to colleagues when they experience success. If you have a blog or videos to promote your professional brand, be sure to re-purpose this information on your Facebook page. These activities keep you and your professional areas of expertise top of mind with your friends and colleagues and this could lead to important career introductions.

Adding the professional slant on your Facebook page doesn't mean compromising who you are. Part of the beauty of Facebook is that it gives you a platform for blending personal and professional messaging to show your authentic self and be memorable to friends, family, colleagues, recruiters, and employers.

CHAPTER 4

Interview Mistakes Straight From American Idol: The Dos and Don'ts of Interviewing

No one is born knowing how to interview. With practice everyone can learn how to interview effectively. This chapter focuses on tips for creating a powerful message of value, fielding a variety of interview questions, and negotiating salary.

Can't Remember the Last Time You Went on a Job Interview?

Does it feel like your last interview was during the Reagan administration? You are not alone. If it's been a long time since your last interview, here are some tips for starting off on the right foot.

1. **Create an interview strategy.** Prepare for interviews by going through the following exercise to reflect on past work accomplishments: Ask yourself what challenges you have faced in each of your positions, what actions you took to address those challenges, and what the corresponding results were. Use past performance reviews, letters of recommendation, and LinkedIn recommendations, and have conversations with colleagues, vendors, and past supervisors to flesh out your unique value proposition. If you are returning to the workforce after being a stay-at-home parent, also do this exercise for any volunteer activities you may have been part of.

2. **Practice.** Proper interview strategy is not something you are born with. Practice will help you crystallize your message and calm pre-interview jitters. Call your voicemail and leave answers to tough interview questions and then playback the message to review the quality of your responses and make appropriate edits. Or ask a friend or colleague to videotape a mock interview to help you prepare for the real thing.

3. **Audit your wardrobe and update your interview attire,** particularly if you previously worked in a business casual environment.

4. **Update your computer skills** if you feel you may be lacking in this area or have become rusty on these skills following a stint at home. This doesn't require a large financial investment. A student can often help you quickly beef up your skills.

5. **Get out and meet people.** Join professional organizations for your industry and/or job function and leverage online business networking tools such as LinkedIn to find people in your field.

6. **Benchmark your salary.** If you have been out of the market for some time, your last salary may not represent competitive market value. If you have been out of the workforce for some time, your past salary will provide few clues to your current earning power. Talk to professionals in your industry and recruiters to uncover information on salary ranges in your field and supplement this information by reviewing salary benchmarking sites such as Salary.com and Payscale.

7. **Anticipate obstacles.** Hiring managers may be resistant to a candidate who has been with the same company for 20 years or has been out of the workforce for 10 years. Have stories of success ready that show that while you were with one company for a long time, you held different roles, worked for many different people, or went through business process changes that required you to be flexible and manage change. If you are returning to work, focus on the skills acquired during your time away from corporate America that have allowed you to grow and are important to a prospective employer's current business needs.

Focus on the Things You Can Control

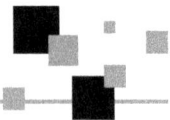

The interview process can be extremely subjective. You can't make people like you or force them to think you are the best fit for the job. Some aspects of interviewing and landing a job just aren't in your control. Rather than second guessing yourself or feeling defeated, examine your interview strategy and make note of what could be improved in the future.

While you can't control every aspect of the interview, you certainly can control the way you prepare for an interview. By being prepared and ready to showcase strong stories of success and a compelling value proposition, there is a greater likelihood that you will be seen as a strong fit and someone who could quickly contribute to the organization.

One of the best ways to prepare for an interview is to write down all your stories of success in your current and past jobs. Next look for the common themes within these stories of success and identify stories that demonstrate your impact on the business, particularly how you have helped the companies you have supported make money, save money, save time, grow the business, keep the business, or create new product. Next match these stories to potential interview questions and make decisions on which stories you could showcase to prove you have the particular competency the hiring authority is asking about in the interview question.

Remember, when you walk into an interview, you are often an unknown. The hiring manager needs to feel confident that there is little risk in hiring you and that you will be able to get up to speed quickly and perform the job successfully. Strong stories of success help mitigate the risk and make hiring managers feel confident in you and your abilities. Strong stories of success also help strengthen rapport with the hiring manager and increase your "likeability."

Take charge of the parts of the hiring process you can control and don't sweat the things you can't. There will be times when the job is filled internally or the chemistry between you and the hiring manager just isn't there. It happens to everyone. Accept it and move on. Invest your energy in honing your interview skills, creating and maintaining an impeccable online identity campaign, and targeting companies with cultures that are in synch with what is important to you. This combination of research and preparation may help increase the chances of being seen as the perfect fit during your next interview.

Interview Mistakes Straight From American Idol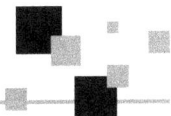

I've always been fascinated by American Idol because it is like watching one really long job interview unfold over several months. Every season, contestants make the same classic interview mistakes. Here are a few of the more painful ones to watch.

1. **Expecting job interest to make up for lack of experience.** How many times have we heard a contestant say, "If you just put me through to the next round, I won't disappoint you. I will work hard and I know I can meet your expectations." But these contestants, like job seekers, rarely get through to the next round unless they can quickly prove during round one that they are a good fit for the position and that they have transferable skills and relevant success stories.

2. **Failure to research the company.** One of my favorite questions that the judges often ask is, "Have you seen this show before?" They ask this to people who appear clueless regarding the level of the competition and the expectations for future American Idols based on the caliber of their predecessors. Likewise, job seekers need to understand the history and culture of the organization they are interviewing with to determine the likelihood of meeting their selection criteria and being perceived as a good fit.

3. **Confusion over the job role.** Every year there are always a few contestants that are dancers, comedians, or actors...but not singers. They basically ignore the job description and go into the audition showing off what they can do, even if it is incongruous to what the judges are looking for. I see this same tactic used in the job search world; it manifests itself as the job seeker who applies to any position, regardless of the position's relevance to their skill set. This strategy rarely works and it can damage your credibility as a legitimate candidate. If you are applying for specific opportunities, you should only apply to those where your skill set matches numerous requirements as specified on the job posting.

4. **Inappropriate dress.** Once a girl showed up for the audition in a bikini. She did this to be different, garner attention from the judges, and possibly distract them from her mediocre voice. While it's true that she got through (Randy and Simon couldn't say no), she didn't get past round two. During an interview, you want to be remembered for what you said, not for what you wore.

What Not to Wear to the Interview

Every year after the big celebrity awards shows, the pundits weigh in on the best and worst dressed of the evening. While an interview isn't quite the same as a walk down the red carpet, hiring authorities are paying attention to what candidates wear to job interviews. Here are some of the biggest fashion mistakes I see job seekers make.

Women

1. **Long fingernails** with bright or distracting nail polish. Nails should be clipped short and it is recommended that you wear clear or light polish.

2. **Short skirts.** Make sure you can sit and cross your legs comfortably. If your teenage daughter thinks your skirt is the right length, it is probably too short.

3. **Too much jewelry.** Multiple bangle bracelets can be noisy and distracting during an interview. Only wear one pair of earrings (and only in your ears).

4. **Too much perfume.** An overpowering scent can quickly turn a one-hour interview into a 20-minute interview. Go easy on the perfume or skip it altogether.

5. **Inappropriate footwear.** It is fine to wear a shoe with a heel, but stay away from stilettos and open-toed shoes.

6. **Big Hair.** If you plan to wear your hair down, try to keep it off your face. Otherwise, opt for a neat style that pulls the hair away from your face.

Men

1. **Unruly facial hair.** Clean shaven is preferred. If you have a moustache or a beard, get a trim before the interview.

2. **Long Hair.** Off the face and ears is best.

3. **Unkempt fingernails.** Nails should be trimmed and clean.

4. **Too much cologne.** Same reasons as stated for women.

5. **Unpolished Shoes.** It's not just about having a nice suit. Clean, polished shoes complete the look.

6. **Lose Change.** Jostling change in your pocket can be noisy and distracting. Clear out your pockets before the interview.

By choosing styles that are appropriate for your age, industry, and professional brand you can ensure that your candidacy is judged on your accomplishments, rather than what you wear to the interview.

Look for Clues to Uncover the Corporate Culture

I often remind my clients that when they are interviewing for an open position they are interviewing the employer as much as the employer is interviewing them. By paying attention to the subtle clues in the office environment, job seekers can gain a better perspective on the culture of the company or division they are interviewing with and make more informed decisions regarding fit. Here are a few tips to help you size up the work environment of the company you are interviewing with.

1. **If possible, schedule your interview early in the morning, late in the day, or during lunchtime.** When you arrive, look around and see whom else is there at that time. If you have an early morning or early evening appointment and the office is packed, chances are that the culture is one that necessitates coming in early or staying late. If you interview during lunch and everyone seems to be eating at their desk, that too could be a clue about the culture of the organization. If you are interviewing with a company that has a company parking lot, observe how full the lot is during these hours to determine if late nights or early mornings are part of the culture of the entire organization.

2. **Ask to do a walk-through of the office.** If you have made it to the second round of interviews, consider asking to see the office space. This allows you to canvas the physical space but again gives you important clues about the office culture. Is the set up cubicle style, big open spaces, windowed offices, or a lot of closed doors? Does the space appear clean and well maintained and a place where you would feel comfortable and safe?

3. **Make small talk with the receptionist.** This is important for several reasons. Many hiring authorities ask the receptionist their impressions of candidates that come in to apply for jobs. Make sure their first impression of you is positive. Through your conversation, you may gain valuable tidbits of information or see firsthand what types of people come through the reception area and how they interact with each other.

4. **Note any interruptions during the interview.** Again, this could be a sign of what it's like to work in that particular environment. Did your interview start on time or were you kept waiting? Is the interview conducted in a quiet environment behind closed doors? Does the person interviewing you interrupt the flow of the meeting to take phone calls? Does the interview end abruptly due to some sort of office crisis? While there are some hiring authorities that "stage" interruptions to see how you deal with them, I truly believe that for the most part these are not planned, but instead are indicative of the department's culture or the hiring manager's style.

Of course, nothing is perfect and I'm not suggesting that you penalize a company or hiring authority for a misstep. However, I do think that it is important to observe the rhythm of the office and factor that information into the final decision making process.

Interviews... Get by With a Little Help from Your Friends

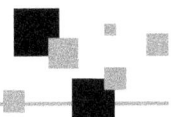

During interviews, hiring managers are looking for clues about a candidate's competency and ability to fit into their work environment. They look for proof of past success as a way to gain confidence in the candidate's abilities and are much less likely to make an offer if the candidate can't deliver this proof. Hiring managers are also interested in what others say about your performance and if you can demonstrate that the people who you connect with in your professional life can consistently articulate your value add, you are more likely to convince them that you are a good fit for their open position.

Here are a few recommendations for incorporating feedback from others into your interview strategy:

1. **Re-read your performance reviews and pay special attention to notes about projects where you helped the company make money, save money, save time, grow the business or keep the business.** Look for examples of how you did more with less, improved a process or completed a project ahead of schedule or under budget.

2. **Talk to colleagues, peers and vendors to see what they say about your performance or relationships with them.** If you are using social networking tools such as LinkedIn or BranchOut, ask for endorsements and use these endorsements in your interview strategy to prove your successes.

3. **Take advantage of a 360-feedback tool.** Checkster has a simple and free tool that you can use to gather collective feedback that is anonymous, confidential and fully automated. Incorporate information about what others say about your performance into your interview strategy to validate your competencies and unique value proposition.

Take a Ride in the Elevator before You Interview

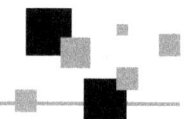

Everyone needs an elevator pitch, which is a quick overview of who you are and the value you can bring to an organization. This overview of your competencies was coined the elevator pitch because the message should be succinct enough to deliver to an important decision maker if you had the chance to ride up in an elevator with him or her.

The elevator pitch is also the perfect response to many interview questions including:

Tell me about yourself.

Walk me through your background.

Why should I hire you?

What can you do that the other 50 candidates cannot?

A strategically crafted elevator pitch will help you answer any of these questions. You should always be ready to deliver your elevator pitch in an exciting and memorable way. Ultimately, you want to be able to recite a message that is clear, targeted, and easy for anyone to understand. When the pitch is presented in this way, you are more likely to create an advocate for your candidacy who can refer your qualifications on to the next appropriate person in the hiring chain. Below are the five key components of an effective elevator pitch.

Create a professional identity.

Select an identity that best relates to your past experiences or future career direction. For some, professional identity is clear-cut. For others it is harder to label. If your identity doesn't exactly match a known profession, create an overall statement of the value you bring to an organization.

Showcase three strengths.

Highlight three areas of competency that show your value add and differentiate you from the competition. Chose traits that can easily be coupled with examples of how you have helped the organizations you have supported make money, save money, save time, maintain the business, or grow the business. For example, being proficient in Microsoft Project can position a project manager as a candidate that gets the job done expeditiously and in turn saves time, money, and resources.

Use accomplishment-focused, metrics-driven examples to support your strengths.

Just like the resume, the pitch must include proof that you have successfully completed job relevant tasks. A good strategy is to marry a strength with a specific example to prove that you are accomplished at what you do. Quantify accomplishments using numbers, percentages, and dollars whenever possible.

Discuss your background as it relates to the target function or industry.

Draw on your past experiences from several positions to solidify the scope of your skill set, show career progression, and build the business case for your candidacy. Also, include relevant education such as a job-related or advanced degree, industry certifications, advanced technologies, or leadership roles within a professional organization to showcase the diversity of your experiences and position you as a unique contributor.

Make a match between your experience and the skills needed for a particular job function or industry.

Bring the conversation full circle by relating your traits back to the needs of the employer or the needs of a particular industry. By doing so, you prove relevancy and demonstrate why your skills are a good fit for a certain type of position.

Try to craft one pitch that is under a minute and another that is more like a quick tagline. After all, you never know if your decision maker is taking a ride up to the 50th floor or the 5th floor.

What Your Grandparents Can Teach You about Interviewing

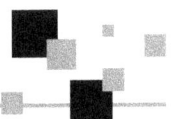

Once I attended a workshop on storytelling. During the workshop, I learned how to tell a better story and be a better listener.

One of the most memorable exercises of the day was when each person in the group was asked to tell a story about one of their grandparents, told through the voice of that grandparent. It was somewhat challenging at first...having to piece together memories that are somewhat hazy now that these people are no longer with me. We were asked to speak for several minutes and I wasn't sure I would have enough to say. I'm sure others in the group felt the same way. But I think we were all surprised by how vivid our memories were and the strong emotions that came out when we told our stories.

There were fascinating stories about grandparents who were immigrants and others impacted by the Great Depression. There were stories of incredible opportunity and incredible loss. And in each story there was humor, intrigue, and drama...every story was moving and memorable.

What I gleaned from these stories is that what made them memorable were the details. Some storytellers used descriptive words or imagery to make a certain fact stand out; others used quotes that the grandparent had actually coined, and still others referenced historical events, religion, geography, and favorite family foods to help the listeners feel that they were truly in the presence of these grandparents.

I started thinking about how job seekers can learn to tell more compelling interview stories by drawing parallels between their family stories and their work stories. A person's family history is unique, compelling, and often something people communicate about with passion. Career stories can be equally unique, compelling, and passionate. Here are a few things to consider when creating your stories for answering interview questions.

1. **Personalization equals passion.** A great story of success to showcase during an interview is one that proves your passion. To simply state that you are passionate about building strong sales teams or creating technology infrastructures would sound cliché. But communicating a story about a time that you put your blood, sweat, and tears into a project to get it done on time and on budget would be an authentic and more interesting way to tell your story and make hiring managers feel confident that you could create similar experiences in their organization.

2. **Everyone has a story.** So many job seekers think they have nothing unique to say. "I just did my job; I didn't do anything special," is one of the statements I hear most frequently from job seekers trying to prove the impact of their work. Like your family history, your work history is unique to you. Try to focus on how you did your job effectively and what you do differently than your colleagues or your predecessors in the position.

3. **The specifics of the story are more important than the general facts.** I don't remember all the facts or the time line of every grandparent story I heard that weekend. But for each story I heard, I remember several snippets that best describe that grandparent and even offer clues to their values and way of life. In interviews, most people think they should talk about their skills in general terms, but it is the specific examples of success and the specific metrics behind those stories that prove your impact that the interviewer will remember.

4. **A personal story can represent a universal feeling or experience.** All the grandparent stories I heard were quite different. Yet there were common themes of family, community, love, and loss that everyone could relate to. When you interview, you are attempting to find common ground with the interviewer. You are trying to develop rapport by proving that the things you have achieved in your past positions will help improve their current work environment.

My grandparent story was about my maternal grandfather, Pat. He and my grandmother were married for 60 years and were first generation Americans living in a small town in Pennsylvania famous for its busy train station, Horseshoe Curve, and Malamar cookies. My grandfather taught me how to hit a baseball. He wrote the letter "e" in a special way that I had never seen before that I copied and still use to this day. He loved watermelon with salt (yuck!) and my grandmother's apple pies. There is a lot more to his story, but you can see how the little details can make the story memorable. So, what's your story and how can you be memorable to employers?

How to Stand Out in a Panel Interview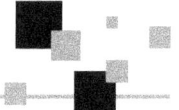

There appears to be a growing trend towards more panel or group interviews and it is becoming increasingly common for job seekers to meet with panels of three or more decision makers in one interview. Here are a few of my own tips on how to survive a panel interview.

1. **When you meet each person on the panel, ask for a business card.** Before the interview begins, place the cards in front of you and facing in the direction of the appropriate person to help you remember the names of the people you are interviewing with. Refer to each person by name during the conversation to personalize your responses and build rapport with the group.

2. **Don't assume that the most senior person is the decision maker.** Frequently business leaders rely on their team to help make decisions about candidates. Be sure to include everyone in the conversation. If one person in the group asks you a question, begin your answer by responding to that person, but then make eye contact with the others to build rapport with everyone in the room.

3. **Try to size up the agenda of everyone in the group.** The needs of the marketing, operations, and sales teams will be different, so make sure you can showcase stories of success that will resonate with the different business heads you are interviewing with.

4. **Send everyone in the group a thank you letter and make sure each letter is unique.** The thank you letter is a great tool for reconnecting with the hiring team, but in order to be seen as authentic, you need to communicate your thanks to each person individually and avoid redundant content. Try to focus on one key point or exchange with each person you interviewed with. It's a bit of extra work, but in the long run, it's worth it.

Mastering the Phone Interview

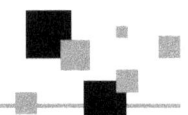

A phone interview should be treated just like any other interview. Here are ten tips for mastering the phone interview.

Schedule the meeting during a time when you won't be distracted.

A phone interview should be scheduled like any other interview. At the designated appointment time, make sure the dog is in the backyard and someone else is watching the kids. If a recruiter or hiring manager calls you without advance notice and wants to interview you on the spot, use caution. If the interview "conditions" are not optimal at the time of the call, it is best to tell the interviewer that you are very interested in the position, but need to schedule another time to have a conversation. That time can be as soon as ten minutes later, just make sure that you can take the call without being distracted.

Conduct interviews from a landline.

Cell phones are a boon to modern communication, but the quality is still not the same as that from a landline. You don't want to frustrate the recruiter or the hiring manager with a bad connection. Plan your interview from a reliable phone line.

Create an office space.

Dedicate an area as your office. This could be as simple as a card table with a phone and your documents. Conduct your interviews from your "office". Being seated at a desk or table allows you to create an environment similar to an in-person interview.

Put a mirror in front of you.

This helps you focus and it anchors your conversation to the visual representation of a person. Monitoring your facial expressions helps you see if you are communicating your enthusiasm to the recruiter.

Have a glass of water nearby.

If your throat is dry or you get a tickle, you can take care of it before it turns into a cough and disrupts the flow of the interview.

Have your notes in front of you.

A phone interview is like an open book test. You can have your company research and answers to potential interview questions right in front of you. Try putting key information on colored index cards and organize by category.

Vary Your Voice.

Since the other person can't see you, it is critical that you vary the tone and cadence of your voice to communicate interest and develop rapport.

Use pauses effectively.

Pauses in an interview situation are always difficult and they can be especially awkward during a phone interview. Rather than wondering what the person on the other end is doing or if they are still there, use the silence to ask a question. For example, if the interviewer has just asked you about your strengths and your response is met with silence, make that an opportunity to ask a question like, "What are the key strengths of your ideal candidate?" This takes care of the silence and allows you to learn more about the position.

Don't multi-task.

We have grown so accustomed to multi-tasking; however, it can be counterproductive during a phone interview. Don't check your email or stick a casserole in the oven while you are engaged in a phone interview. Act the same way you would for an in-office interview and maintain your focus.

Practice.

Record some of your answers to prospective interview questions. Play them back and critique. Are you easy to understand? Is your presentation riddled with long pauses and "ums?" Do you communicate interest and enthusiasm? If necessary, rework your answers and your presentation.

Could Your Interview Style Use a Seven Second Delay?

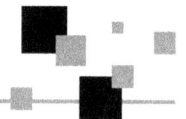

I talk to many job seekers who relay stories of "interviews gone bad" and reveal statements they wish they could take back. But in real interviews (and real life) there is no 7 second delay and that first impression often sticks and plays over and over again in the interviewer's mind.

Here are some things said in interviews that people realize afterwards would be better left unsaid.

What is your biggest weakness?

Candidates often respond by saying they are a perfectionist, thinking this answer actually positions them well by showing their diligence. Not so. Most hiring managers interpret the "I'm a perfectionist" response as "I can't get stuff done." Focus on a "forgivable" weakness that won't be a deal breaker in the new job. Discuss a competency that was part of your last job role but won't play a large part in the new job.

What did you accomplish in your last job that you are most proud of?

Sometimes candidates focus on a situation that was a great success but has little relevance to the role the new employer is trying to fill. Showcase an authentic success but pick one that will still resonate with the needs of the employer.

Tell me about yourself.

Job seekers often respond by telling employers they are motivated, hard working, great communicators, blah, blah, blah. They think this is what employers want to hear (and who can blame them; employers use these words ad nauseam on job specs and wonder why they can't find the right candidate). Focus on competencies and tangible skills, not personal attributes. For every competency you claim to have, offer an example of how you have used that competency to accomplish something for an employer.

Why did you leave your last job?

It can be so tempting to tell the whole story...the one about the unreasonable boss, the boss who you suspect let you go so he could bring in someone cheaper, the corporate politics that you had no control over. Keep your response short and sweet.

If you were laid off, explain the business reasons why the position was eliminated. If you left on your own or were asked to leave, discuss a change in the direction of the department, business objectives, etc. Keep the conversation focused on the business reasons and not the personalities.

Since you will never have the luxury of a 7 second delay during a job interview, the best preparation strategy is to practice. Write out all your stories of success beforehand and make some decisions about which stories to showcase for certain types of questions. While you don't want to sound stiff and rehearsed, having some sort of a script is a sound strategy and will help you avoid saying something that you can't take back.

Common Interview Questions and What They Mean

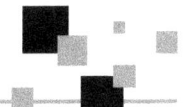

Have you ever wondered why an interviewer asks certain interview questions? Some of the questions seem so vague and random that it can be hard to figure out the logic behind the interview process. What's right? What's wrong? What does the hiring manager really want to hear? Below is a quick guide to the translations for some of the most common interview questions.

Question: Tell me about yourself.

Translation: Why should I hire you?

Recommended response. Don't take the question too literally. Hiring managers don't want to hear that you grew up on a small farm in Kansas or that you enjoy world travel. Furthermore, they don't want to hear that you are a great communicator, team player, and fast learner. They want you to show tangible proof of why you would be a good fit for their organization. Outline two to four of your key competencies and couple each competency with proof of success. For example, an operations professional might showcase one of his/her competencies by saying, "I have strong project management skills and can quickly resolve customer inquiries. For example, in my last job, I resolved 98 percent of all pending customer inquiries within 24 hours. This was 50 percent faster than the company's expectation for problem resolution."

Question: What is your weakness?

Translation: We know what your weakness is. Prove to us it's not a liability for this position.

Recommended response. Before your interview address any potential obstacles that the hiring manager may pick up on. Perhaps it is your lack of knowledge with a specific software or your lack of experience in a particular industry. Show how you would overcome these obstacles or demonstrate how you have overcome similar obstacles in the past. For example, if you apply for a position that requires a certain technical skill and you have limited experience, give an example of another software you are proficient in and how you gained that proficiency to prove that your current limited knowledge is a minor liability that can be quickly overcome.

Question: Where do you see yourself in five years?

Translation: Do you have a realistic perspective on what this job/company is about?

Recommended Response. Craft a response that makes sense for the employer's business environment. If it is a small company, don't say you expect to have a position with increasing responsibility — that may not be feasible in their organization. If you are taking a job as an accountant just to get a foot in the door of the company but really want to be a controller, don't bring that up during the interview. The hiring manager needs to know that you are committed to the job you are applying for, not already thinking about a new job. You can mention that you see yourself in a position where you can continue to learn and contribute to the company's bottom line and give an example of how you were able to successfully do that at a previous organization. This answer will help managers feel confident in your level of commitment to the current job and your future commitment to the organization.

Question: What have you been doing since your last position ended?

Translation: Why have you been out of work so long?

Recommended response. Discuss any volunteer or consulting assignments you may have had in the interim. If you have been actively interviewing but haven't been extended an offer, you can mention that you have been interviewing but haven't found the right fit yet. If you have had limited activity, you can let the hiring manager know that you have been using this time to evaluate your skills, craft your resume, conduct informational interviews, and network within professional circles. Obviously, saying you've been watching re-runs of 20 consecutive seasons of 'Law & Order' won't go over well, so stick to discussing the professional activities you have been involved in.

Question: Are you interviewing with other companies?

Translation: Are you worth investing some time in or are you about to take another offer?

Recommended response. Generally, it's best to be somewhat vague in your response, particularly if you are at the beginning of your search. If it is early on, let the employer know that you have just begun the interview process. If you have been in search mode for a while, let them know that you have been actively searching but haven't found the right fit yet.

Question: Tell me about the accomplishment you are most proud of.

Translation: Is your past experience similar to what we need you to do here?

Recommended response. The accomplishment you are most proud of might not be the one that is most relevant to the organization's needs. Showcase an accomplishment that proves you have the specific competencies to do the job they need you to do. The story you select may be different for different interviews. That's all right. You can be proud of more than one accomplishment, and it is more important to showcase the right accomplishment than it is to bring up the achievement that brought you the greatest personal satisfaction.

Question: Tell me about a time when you lacked the appropriate resources to do your job and how you handled it.

Translation: We are severely understaffed *or* we don't have a budget for anything.

Recommended response. Give an example that proves that you have been in this situation before and that you can do more with less. But if you notice this is a running theme throughout the interview, proceed with caution. You could be setting yourself up to assume an impossible role with very limited support.

Question: How many golf balls can fit in a school bus?

Translation: Are you analytical, how do you solve problems, *or* do you mind if we just want to mess with your head?

Recommended Response. This type of question is often referred to as a brainteaser. Interviewers don't expect you to know the answer, but they will want to see how you tackle figuring out a strategy to come up with an answer. These questions tend to be most popular in high-tech companies, but job candidates in other industries sometimes get them as well.

How to Handle "Inappropriate" Interview Questions

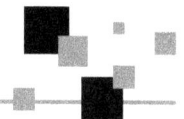

I frequently hear stories from job seekers about inappropriate or illegal questions that they are asked during an interview. I can understand why these questions would frustrate job seekers. But often hiring managers ask questions that are "just plain wrong" because of their agenda, because of a concern they have about your candidacy or a fear of finding something problematic about you after they have hired you. In many cases, the inappropriate question is asked without even realizing it is inappropriate or even illegal. So before you get defensive about a certain question, try to examine the hiring manager's motive behind asking it. Below are a few inappropriate interview questions along with the potential motive for asking them and suggested responses.

Are you married? Clearly, this is an inappropriate question and marital status has nothing to do with your success in the position. But the motive behind asking the question may be the fear that if you are married, you may be planning on starting a family soon, which could mean an extended leave or even a decision to quit. But rather than getting defensive about the question, try answering it by acknowledging the motive. Respond by saying something like, "If you are concerned that my marital status could affect my long term plans at the company, I can assure you that is not the case."

How many children do you have? Absolutely, politically incorrect? Sure. But some managers ask this question because they are concerned that if you have kids, you are more likely to come in late or leave early, need more time off, or need a more flexible work schedule. Rather than getting defensive and saying that they are asking an inappropriate question, again try to assuage their fears by understanding their motive and say something like, "If you are concerned that my parental status will affect my ability to carry out all my work duties and be present at all work-related functions on a regular basis, I can assure you that my commitments to the company would not be compromised."

You have an interesting name. Where are you from? Does this question reek of discrimination? Possibly. Or, the employer may be asking this question because they are not sure if you are authorized to work in the U.S. and they cannot offer you a work Visa. You can respond by saying, "If you are concerned about my authorization to work in the U.S. I would be happy to provide you with proof of citizenship (or a green card)."

How old are you? Yes, I've actually had clients who were asked this question during an interview. Offensive? Absolutely. But again, try to examine the underlying motive. Perhaps the hiring manager is concerned that your skills are not current or that they will not be able to afford someone with your level of experience. Rather than getting defensive say something like, "I can assure you that my age has no bearing on my ability to do the job. My skills are up to date and my salary requirements are flexible."

Interviewing is about building a relationship and establishing rapport. Getting defensive never works well in an interview situation. If you later decide that the hiring manager is an absolute Neanderthal for asking you inappropriate or illegal interview questions, you can always decide not to pursue the position. But it's a sounder interview strategy to address the motives behind the questions head on.

Interview Questions for Recent College Grads

Are you prepared for your first interview out of college? Below are four interview questions geared towards recent college graduates.

Why did you choose your college/major?

This question gives you the opportunity to show the hiring manager how you set goals and monitor success. For example, if you chose your university because it has one of the best academic programs in a particular field of study, you probably became interested in this program during high school and made a conscious decision at that time to build a portfolio of academic successes and extracurricular activities that made you a desirable candidate for that college. This shows your commitment to project completion as well as a high tolerance for challenging, competitive situations.

How does your degree prepare you for a career in (industry) or to excel as a (job title)?

The hiring manager is asking you to link your academic major with your targeted positions right after college. Draw on your college experiences including specific curriculum examples, a senior thesis, contributions to class projects, relevant internships, and extracurricular activities to demonstrate parallels between academic success and that expected of you in the world of work.

What qualifications do you have beyond academics that qualify you to make a successful transition into business?

There are two types of extracurricular activities that you can discuss...(1) school-related and community-based activities and (2) working arrangements to finance your education.

Participation in the same school-related activities for all four years validates that a candidate knows their strengths and is choosing to actively pursue them. It also shows a high level of discipline and commitment.

Students who financed their education through part-time and summer jobs can show how these jobs contributed to a strong sense of self-determination and self-reliance. They can make direct correlations between the skills learned on the job and their relevance to the position they are applying for. These students can also show employers how they successfully manage multiple tasks, prioritize responsibilities, and manage their time effectively.

Do you think your grades are a good indicator of your ability to succeed in business?

Grades may reflect an individual's potential performance, but it is not guaranteed. Never apologize for less than stellar grades or blame others for poor performance; this could lead the hiring manager to believe you don't feel confident in your abilities or don't take responsibility for your actions. Instead, try to present a complete picture of your candidacy by discussing your grades within the context of your other accomplishments in college. For example, if you were a B student, but also held a leadership role in your fraternity or worked 30 hours a week to finance your education, let the hiring manager know about these successes.

What is Your Weakness and Other Tough Interview Questions

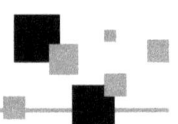

Every job seeker hates interview questions like *what is your weakness* or *tell me about a mistake you made*. Many believe these questions are designed to make them sweat and there can't possibly be a good answer. Others have heard that the key to answering these tough questions is to spin the response and turn a negative into a positive.

However, these responses usually either lack authenticity or are otherwise misguided, since what many people think would be perceived as a strength to the hiring manager is actually considered a liability. Candidates that lack authenticity are easy to spot, and the outcome of the interview is severely compromised when job seekers choose to spin their responses to tough interview questions.

In fact, in a 2009 Society for Human Resources Management survey, recruiters and hiring managers reported that one of their biggest pet peeves within the context of the interview situation was candidates that responded to difficult interview questions with answers that attempted to spin a tough situation into one with only positive outcomes. Below are a few of the most common interview questions that job seekers try to spin their responses to and some suggested alternative responses.

What is your greatest weakness?

Red flag answer

"I am a perfectionist and I get frustrated when people aren't as committed to the job as I am."

Problem

The candidate is answering the question about a weakness by responding with an answer that suggests a strength. Such answers are disingenuous and are not well received by hiring authorities. The candidate is also assuming that perfection is considered a desirable trait in the organization. Some hiring managers will perceive a perfectionist as someone who gets so caught up in the details that they can't achieve the project's objectives.

Adjusted response

Earlier in my career, when I was a software developer, my strong attention to detail was an asset because I could quickly spot and correct systems errors. But, after I was promoted to project manager, this strength became a bit of a liability because I was now responsible for delegating work and overseeing the big picture aspect of the project. I struggled at first because it was my nature to want to fix every error. While I still have that tendency, I now rely on the technical expertise of my team and this allows me to concentrate on delivering projects on time and on budget.

Tell me about a situation where you did not get along with a supervisor.

Red flag answer

"I've been very fortunate, and I've never worked for someone I didn't get along with."

Problem

Everyone has had situations where they disagreed with a boss, and by saying you have not, you force the interviewer to question your integrity. It also can send out a signal that the candidate is not seasoned enough or hasn't been in situations that require him to develop a tough skin or deal with confrontation.

Adjusted response

"It's natural for people to have differing opinions. When this has occurred in the past, I have presented my reasons for my position and openly listened to my supervisor's opinion as well. Recently, my supervisor recommended a change to a report that in my opinion made the reporting more cumbersome and time-consuming. I expressed my concerns but also asked many questions to determine what information my boss needed to capture what was not currently in the report. Once I understood her needs, I was able to offer a suggestion that satisfied her information needs and actually streamlined the existing report and made it easier to use."

Describe a situation where an initiative you were part of failed.

Red flag answer

"I've never had a project that failed; my supervisors have always praised my work."

Problem

If you can't discuss a failure or mistake, the interviewer might conclude that you do not possess the depth of experience necessary to do the job. The interviewer is not looking for perfection. They are trying to better understand your level of responsibility, your decision-making process, your ability to recover from a mistake, what you learned from the experience, and if you can take responsibility for your mistakes.

Adjusted response

"Everyone makes mistakes. I'd like to think that I have learned something valuable from every mistake I have made. In my previous role as marketing director, I launched a product and was disappointed in the initial sales results. I realized that we had launched too quickly and needed to do additional market research to determine the needs of multiple demographics within our market. Following the research initiative, the marketing was realigned with a niche demographic and sales doubled within one year."

By developing and practicing responses to difficult interview questions that display honesty, thoughtfulness, good will, and fallibility, you will create a realistic and authentic portrait of your candidacy and develop a strong rapport with the hiring authority. This will help you advance to the next round in the interview process and lead you one step closer to securing the position.

24 Interview Tips That Help Make a Great First Impression

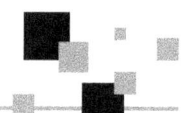

Many think that some people are natural interviewees and that those with outgoing personalities will surely do better in an interview. But with practice everyone can learn how to interview effectively. Here are some quick interview tips for creating a more powerful interview strategy.

1. Your interview starts the moment you walk into the building; anyone you meet may be connected with the hiring manager or the hiring team.

2. Be nice to everyone you meet from the receptionist up to the senior-level executives; everyone's opinion counts.

3. Your elevator pitch is a quick overview of who you are and the value you can bring to an organization.

4. Craft one pitch you could deliver riding up to the 50th floor of the elevator and another for a ride up to the fifth floor.

5. Practice your elevator pitch by calling your voice mail and recording your spiel; play back the message to determine what needs editing.

6. When asked why you are in job search, say something positive about the current or past employer first, then explain your reason for looking.

7. If you were downsized, explain the business reason why you were let go. Don't personalize the situation -- it wasn't about you.

8. If interviewing with several people at the same time, give everyone equal attention; you never know who the real decision maker is.

9. When participating in a phone interview always use a landline and don't put your phone on speaker.

10. Answer interview questions by communicating strong stories of success; prove what makes you unique rather than just explaining what you did.

11. Try to ask questions throughout the interview; it should be a conversation not an interrogation.

12. Asking questions during the interview helps you uncover key issues and better prepares you to answer questions throughout the interview.

13. Be sure to ask what the next steps in the interview process are so you can prepare an appropriate follow-up strategy.

14. Create a brief and visually interesting presentation about your skills and achievements to give to the hiring manager during the interview.

15. When asked questions about mistakes you have made, be authentic, explain what you learned from the experience, and don't get defensive.

16. If asked about your weaknesses, don't spin weaknesses into strengths; it's not credible and who wants to hire someone they don't trust?

17. Ask big-picture questions about the company and how the department you are interviewing with fits into the company's long-term goals.

18. People think they should talk in general terms about career successes, but you build trust with interviewers by talking about specifics.

19. If recruiters ask you to "walk them through your background," focus on your core message of value, not the five positions you held pre-1985.

20. Interviewees are a risk to hiring managers because they don't know you. Prove success that can be duplicated in their company to earn trust.

21. A good interviewee is also a good listener. The questions asked provide clues to what the hiring manager needs and expects.

22. If you are the No. 2 candidate for a job, stay in contact with the company; many follow their "silver medalists" and recruit them later on.

23. Hang out in the company lobby the day before your interview to see how people dress; then dress at least one level up from that.

24. For lunch interviews, pass on the alcohol, garlic, and messy foods; and don't order the most expensive item on the menu.

6 Tips for Following Up after the Interview

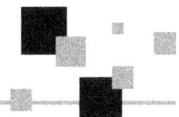

The time in between an interview and decisions for the next round of interviews can feel like an eternity when you are anxious to move your job search forward. What can you do in conjunction with the interview process to follow up strategically and intelligently? Here are a few suggestions.

1. During the interview, ask when the hiring manager plans to conduct the next round of interviews or make the job offer.

If you ask this question during the interview, you are more likely to have some sort of benchmark to go by for follow-up, and the waiting game becomes more manageable. If you are told that the company plans to get back to all applicants in one week, then it would certainly be acceptable to call on day eight if you haven't heard from the company and remind them that they mentioned giving candidates a status update in one week and you are just checking in.

2. Send a thank you letter.

A thank you letter is more than just a courtesy. It's an opportunity to remind the hiring manager of the value you can bring to the organization. Some candidates don't bother sending a thank you letter; doing so can be another way to differentiate you.

3. Ask if you can stay in touch with the hiring manager during the interview period.

Sometimes a company's plans for filling a position can be extended, particularly if it is a large company or if you are interviewing at a company where there isn't a live job opening. In these cases, it is important to remain top of mind with the hiring authority. You can say, "I know you won't be making a decision for some time, but I would like to stay in touch." Or, "Can I send you a LinkedIn invitation? That way we can stay in touch during this interim period."

4. Continue to research company openings and movement.

If the position was posted on the company website or a job board, continue to monitor the posting to see if it was closed or removed. Priorities in companies can change quickly and by monitoring the status of the posting, you may gain clues as to what is happening internally in the organization.

5. Stay in touch with company contacts.

If you got the interview through a networking lead, stay connected with that person to see whether they have any knowledge of what's going on in the organization. Perhaps the hiring manager has decided to add additional positions or upgrade the job to which you applied .

6. Be patient.

We'd like to think that we are the first thing on the hiring manager's mind, but usually we aren't. Interviewing is generally just one small part of the hiring manager's responsibility — and sometimes unfortunately, it takes a back seat to other pressing issues.

If after all the waiting, it turns out that you are not the person selected for the position, don't abandon the relationship you worked so hard to create; just reinvent it. Find opportunities to stay in touch with the hiring manager. Many companies like to keep in touch with their No. 2 choice for the position because there might be a better fit for that person somewhere down the line. Every hiring manager you meet can turn into a networking contact and a possible resource for the future.

6 Strategies for Gathering Salary Information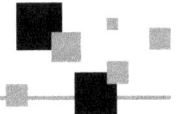

Trying to gather some competitive data on salaries for a particular job function? Here are six strategies you can use to gather important salary information. Knowing your market value before you start interviewing will help you craft a sound negotiation strategy later on if you are selected for the position.

1. **Speak to industry contacts.** They may be able to shed light on salary ranges for positions in various industries and at various professional levels.

2. **Review job postings.** Many job boards list salary ranges; this information can help you decipher the going market value for similar jobs.

3. **Contact recruiters and professional associations in your field to benchmark positions.** Recruiters will know what the market will bear based on recent placements. Professional associations may have survey data to help you better understand your market value.

4. **Refer to salary sites** such as Payscale, Salary.com, and Glassdoor. Payscale combines salary report data and scrubbed self-reported data to create salary ranges for various positions across multiple industries and geographies. Salary.com pulls information from salary sites used by many HR departments, and Glassdoor culls self-reported salary data.

5. **Be aware that every job has unique factors such as geography and industry that influence salary level.** If you are an IT professional in financial services and you are seeking an IT position in a not-for-profit, chances are the salary range will be lower. If you were working as an analyst in Columbus, Ohio, and you are now seeking a similar position in Boston, Mass., chances are salaries will be higher.

6. **Try to determine the flexibility of the employer you are dealing with.** Is it a large company with strict salary ranges or a smaller company that determines salaries on a case-by-case basis? Knowing this ahead of time can help you figure out how much wiggle room you will have during the negotiation phase.

5 Suggestions for Better Salary Negotiation Conversations

Sometimes people undervalue themselves and this leads to a reluctance to negotiate once there is a job offer on the table. Often they make decisions about salary based on what they feel they need rather than what the market will bear. Here are five tips for better salary negotiation conversations.

1. **Base your salary expectations on what the market will bear** rather than on what you earned in a previous position. All a salary suggests is what someone was willing to pay you at a particular time. Past salary generally has little relevance to your current market value.

2. **Discuss your salary expectations in terms of what is fair and reasonable.** Don't ask for a certain salary because that is what you think you need to earn in order to pay your rent. Instead give an explanation for why the salary you are requesting is directly correlated to the value you will bring to the organization.

3. **Uncover your competition.** Before there is an offer on the table, ask the interviewer questions such as, "Can you tell me where you are in the hiring

process?" or "How many people are you interviewing for this position?" to try to determine how many people you may be competing against for the position. If you discover that you are their only current candidate, you will have more leverage during the negotiation process and may be able to command a higher salary.

4. **Think outside the box and be flexible.** If an employer can't offer you the base compensation you had hoped for, maybe they can offer you a compelling performance bonus, a signing bonus or additional stock options.

5. **Do your homework.** Review salary benchmarking sites to help determine your market value, calculate the value of your benefits package and assess the overall quality of your offer. Supplement this research with conversations with recruiters and industry professionals to further validate the accuracy of your findings.

7 Tips for Salary Negotiation

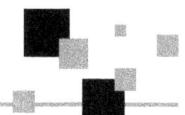

In the job offer context, negotiation is a non-confrontational, business-focused discussion aimed at resolving differences between two parties with the same goal. In order to be an effective negotiator, job seekers need to understand the dynamics behind the conversation and use this information to create a give and take dialogue with potential employers. What often gets in the way of rewarding win-win conversations is our fear of rejection or potential conflict. Successful negotiators view the process as one of collaboration. They listen to the employer's needs and recommend outcomes that benefit both parties. They recognize that savvy negotiators build relationships and never give ultimatums. Strategic job seekers understand that the negotiation is hopefully the first of many relationship building conversations they will have with their future employer. Here are tips the help you become a better negotiator.

Everyone is capable of negotiating. Nobody is born knowing how to be an effective negotiator. It is a learned skill that is developed with experience. We can all learn to negotiate effectively for what we need and want. Keep in mind you wouldn't be receiving the offer in the first place if you weren't the person selected as the best candidate for the job. This gives you leverage. Once an employer decides you are the person for the job, the primary concern will not be to negotiate the least expensive compensation package the company can get away with. The focus will be on getting you to accept the job. Most employers invest a great deal of time and energy in the interview process, and are very reluctant to settle for second best when their number one candidate makes an attempt in good faith to negotiate for more money.

Never ignore job openings because of perceived salary shortcomings. In many cases, those who keep an open mind and interview for positions that at first glance might appear too junior, can build a great deal of value into their candidacy by discussing additional responsibilities they can handle within the position and in turn negotiate a better compensation package.

Always approach a job opportunity like it is the job of your dreams. While you don't want to waste your time to get an offer if you just don't think the job is right for you, many people drop out of the running too early in the interview process because they don't want to be in a position where they have to turn an offer down.

Continue to interview for all but the most unlikely positions until you get the job offer. It's all right to walk away if after the negotiations, the job still isn't a good fit for you. In addition, statistically, one out of every two jobs will be newly created positions in this decade and the next. This allows candidates to help design their own positions with employers throughout the interview and offer process.

Surveys suggest that 85-90% of hiring managers do not make their best offer first. The employer begins the negotiation process knowing how much money is budgeted for the position and how much flexibility there is around that figure. They also know how long they've been looking and how competitive the job market is for someone with your abilities. These factors influence what they offer initially. They want to have some wiggle room... they know the candidate may chose to negotiate their compensation. By starting low, they have built in flexibility during the negotiation process.

Counteroffers are generally 10-15% above the original offer. Again, employers know they may need to negotiate, so it's reasonable to assume that there's flexibility built in to the initial offer. Employers expect you to negotiate. In addition to the financial rewards associated with salary negotiation, you will gain the respect of the hiring manager and increase your credibility within the organization.

Negotiation starts the moment you submit your resume and continues during the interview process. Don't sell yourself at one level and then expect an offer for a higher level. During the interview process, you start building the relationship with the employer and showcasing your value as a candidate. Once you've built maximum value throughout the interview process, you will have the leverage to negotiate the best compensation package possible.

Generally, it is reasonable to request up to one week to make your decision regarding a position. In fact, you should never accept a position on the spot. You want the employer to view you as a prudent decision maker and you want them to understand that you don't rush into big decisions. Express your excitement regarding the offer, but allow yourself some time to think about the level of responsibility within the position and the associated compensation. Another reason for not accepting the offer on the spot is to make sure you have time to review the offer and determine what points you may want to negotiate.

Show Me the Money!

Do you want to negotiate a salary increase this year but are unsure of how you would justify it? Here are some strategies you can implement now to build a strong case for the raise you want in the future.

Document your accomplishments regularly throughout the year

Keep track of all the projects you manage. Upon completion of each assignment, write a note to yourself detailing your contribution and how your efforts helped the company make money, save money, save time, grow the business, or retain customers. Quantify your accomplishments with dollars, percentages, and other appropriate metrics. Actively seek out opportunities to improve efficiencies and profits regardless of the task at hand. By showing and quantifying your specific value add, you build a better business case to support the requested salary increase.

Become hard to replace

Create opportunities to diversify your experience by offering to learn how to perform tasks that support your main role and make you more efficient at what you do. An alternative strategy is to become a subject matter expert in one specific aspect of the job so you are seen as the "go-to-guy" for a particular type of information. No want wants to lose the "go-to-guy" because then they have to do it themselves.

Take on tasks that no one else wants to do

This does not mean taking on grunt work. It might just mean mastering a new technology that no one else feels comfortable with or taking on an assignment that is outside of the traditional scope of the job. Employees who demonstrate this level of flexibility tend to get more flexibility from their bosses on other issues, including compensation.

Accept high profile assignments close to review time

Since it is easier for people to remember what has happened most recently, why not take on an important assignment to coincide with an upcoming review? The project is bound to become a focal point of the performance review discussion and the boss can quickly remember and document the achievements relevant to the project.

Your success negotiating a salary increase or promotion hinges on your ability to discuss the increase in terms of what is fair and reasonable. By including some of these ideas into your career management strategy, you can keep the conversation focused on measureable achievements and build a compelling business case for the requested pay raise.

About the Author

Barbara Safani is the owner of Career Solvers, which partners with Fortune 1,000 companies and individuals to deliver career transition programs focusing on resume development, job search strategies, networking, interviewing, salary negotiation skills, and online identity management.

Barbara has been a career expert for CNN.com, CareerBuilder, and AOL Jobs and she has been quoted extensively in major media outlets, including CBS, ABC, FOX, *The New York Times*, *The Wall Street Journal*, *The Washington Post*, *The LA Times*, *Fortune Magazine*, *Smart Money Magazine*, *Money Magazine*, *Oprah Magazine*, and *Cosmopolitan*.

She is the author of *Happy About My Resume: 50 Tips for Building a Better Document to Secure a Brighter Future, #JOBSEARCH tweet Book01, #SUCCESSFUL CORPORATE LEARNING tweet Book04,* and *Winning Negotiation Strategies for Your New Job.*

Other Happy About® Books

Purchase these books at Happy About http://happyabout.com or at other online and physical bookstores.

Happy About My Resume

The book is for anyone who wants to proactively manage their career and improve the quality of their current resume or create a resume from scratch.

Paperback: $19.95
eBook: $14.95

#JOBSEARCHtweet Book01

#JOBSEARCHtweet' provides job seekers and career advisors proven strategies for job search success in today's competitive job market.

Paperback: $19.95
eBook: $14.95

Other Happy About® Books

Purchase these books at Happy About http://happyabout.com or at other online and physical bookstores.

I'm at a Networking Event -Now What???

'I'm at a Networking Event—Now What???' helps you successfully build networks and connections for your employment, business or social purposes.

Hardcover: $25.46
eBook: $14.95

I Need to Brand My Story Online and Offline-Now What???

If you want to impress someone with your bio and your story, you need to read this book.

Paperback: $22.95
eBook: $16.95

www.ingramcontent.com/pod-product-compliance
Lightning Source LLC
Chambersburg PA
CBHW070801100426
42742CB00012B/2211